Real World

Colouring Book

For Advanced Users & Adults

50 Images

**Created From Real Life Photos
For You To Colour As You Please.**

ISBN 978-0-359-97217-3

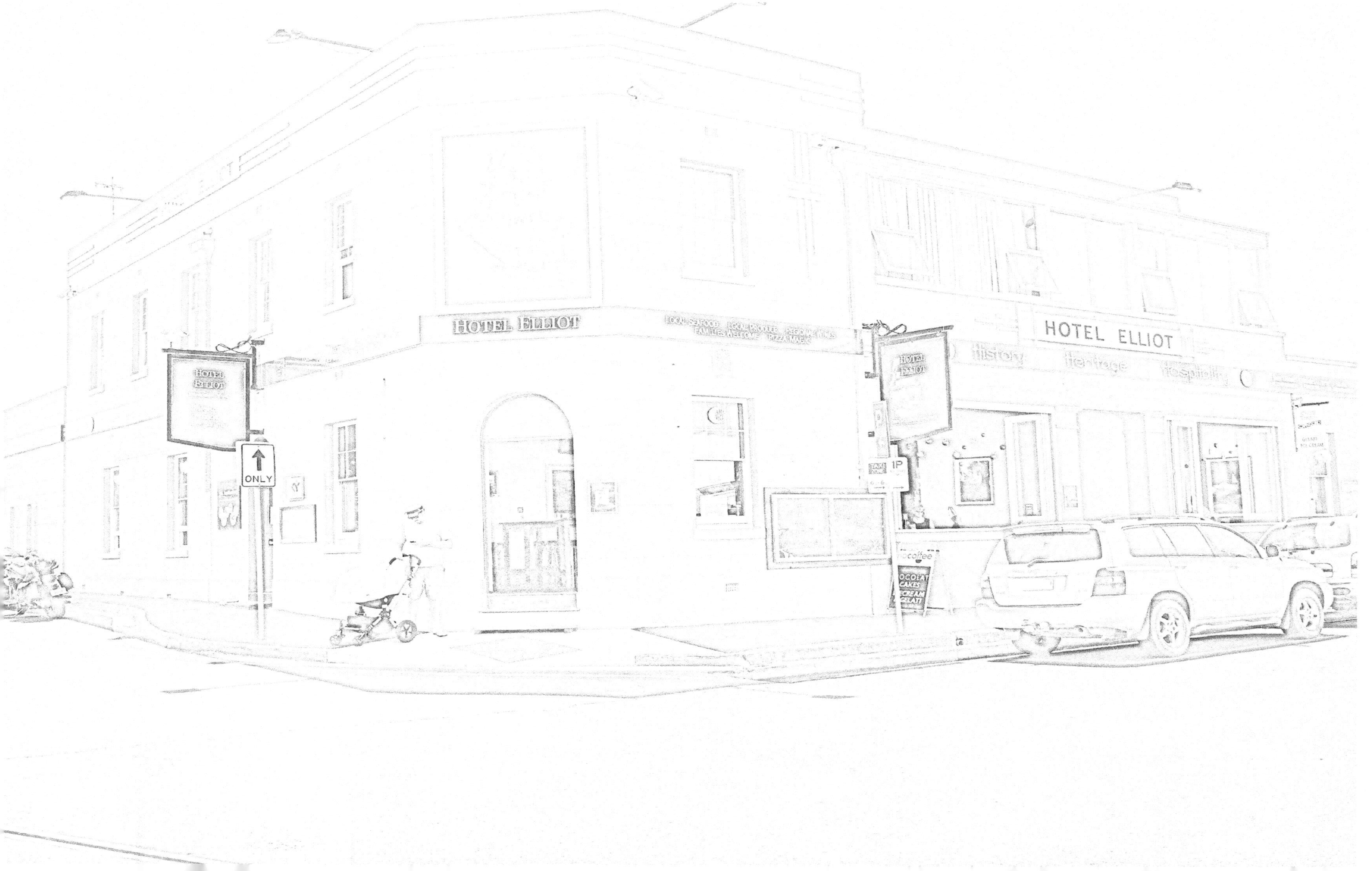
HOTEL ELLIOT
HOTEL ELLIOT
ONLY
HOTEL ELLIOT
HOTEL ELLIOT
history
heritage
hospitality
1P
coffee

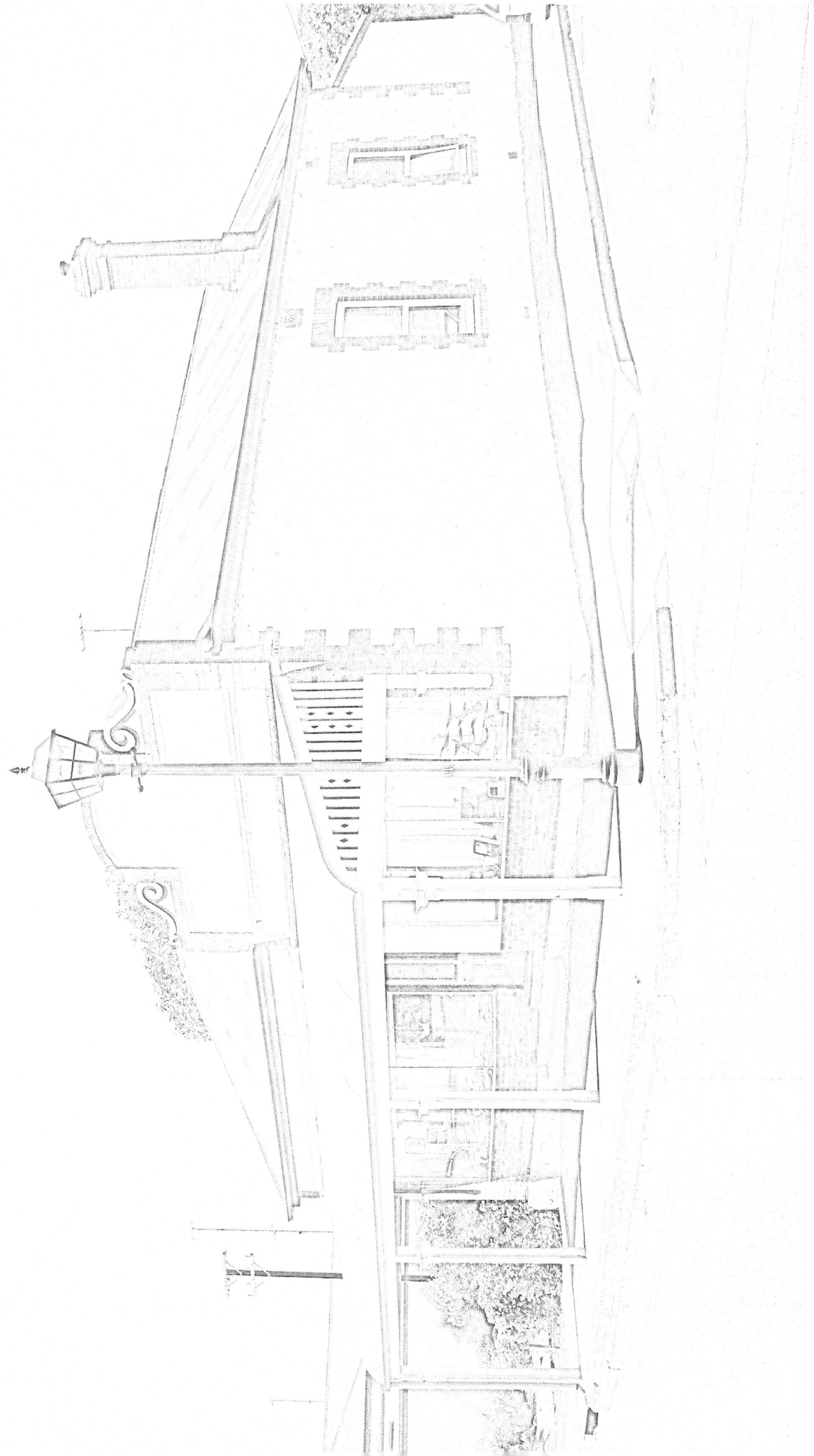

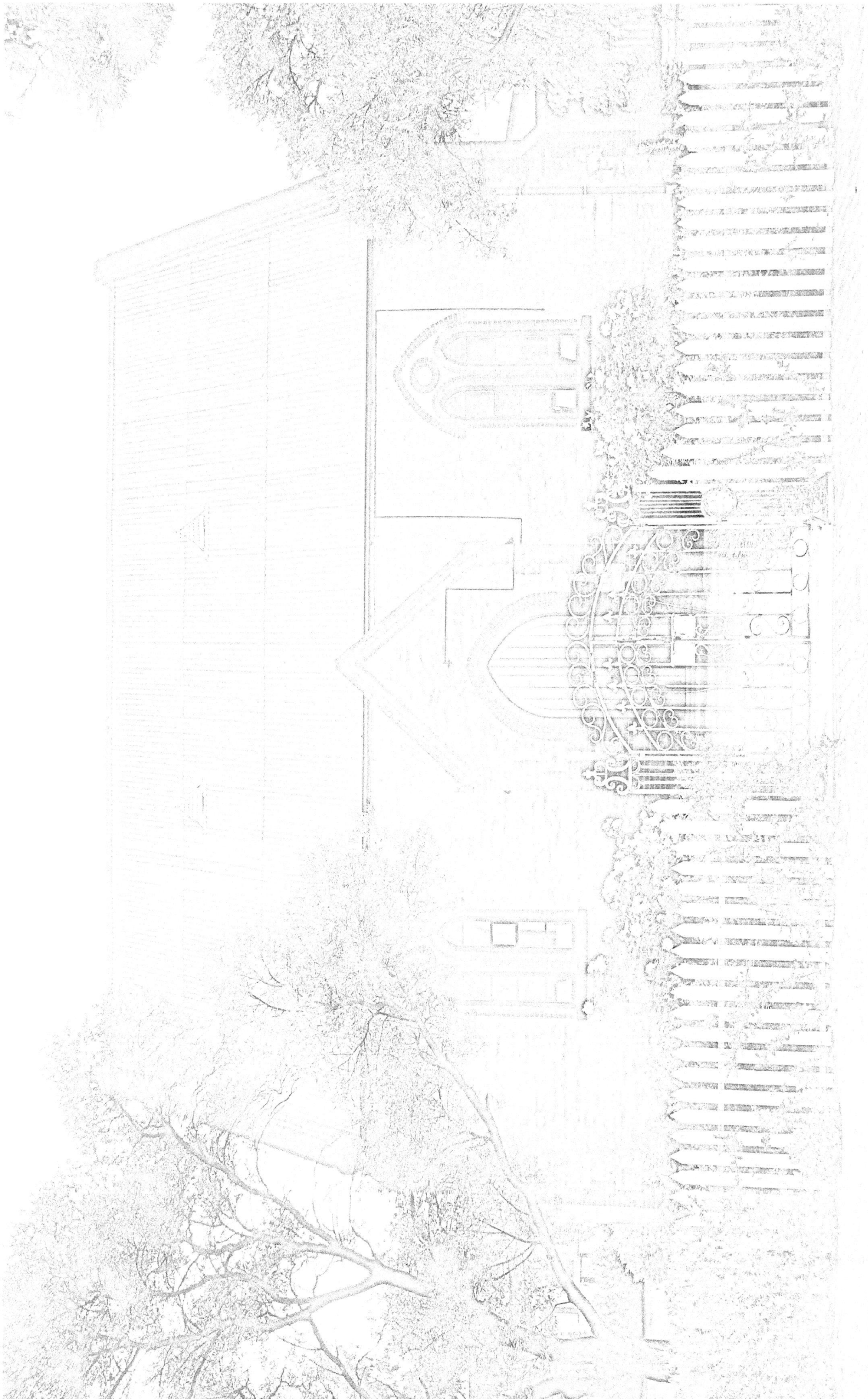

ANTIQUES

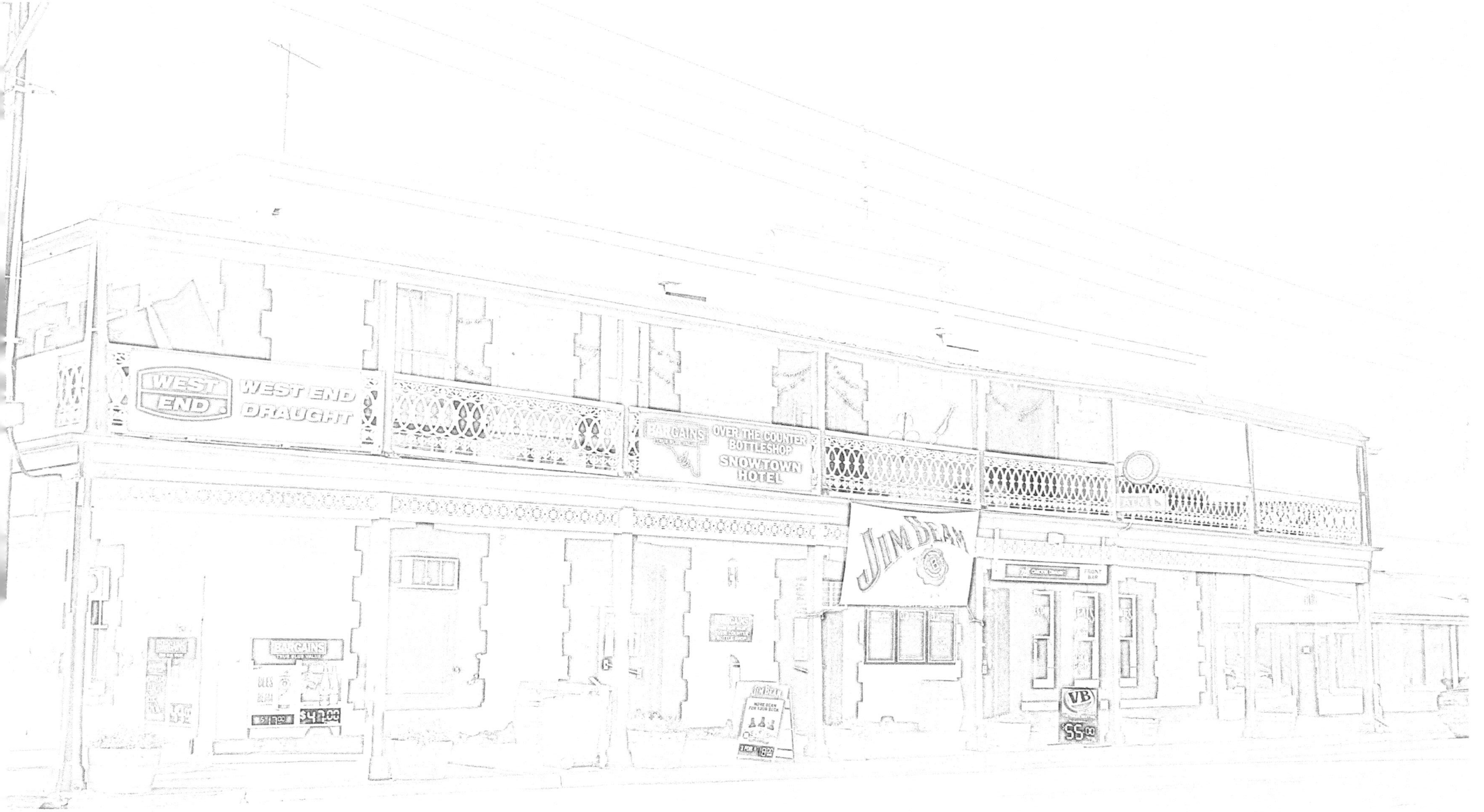
WEST END
WEST END DRAUGHT
BARGAINS
OVER THE COUNTER BOTTLESHOP
SNOWTOWN HOTEL
JIM BEAM
FRONT BAR
VB
$55.00
BARGAINS
$47.00
MORE BEAN FOR YOUR BUCK
3 FOR $18.00

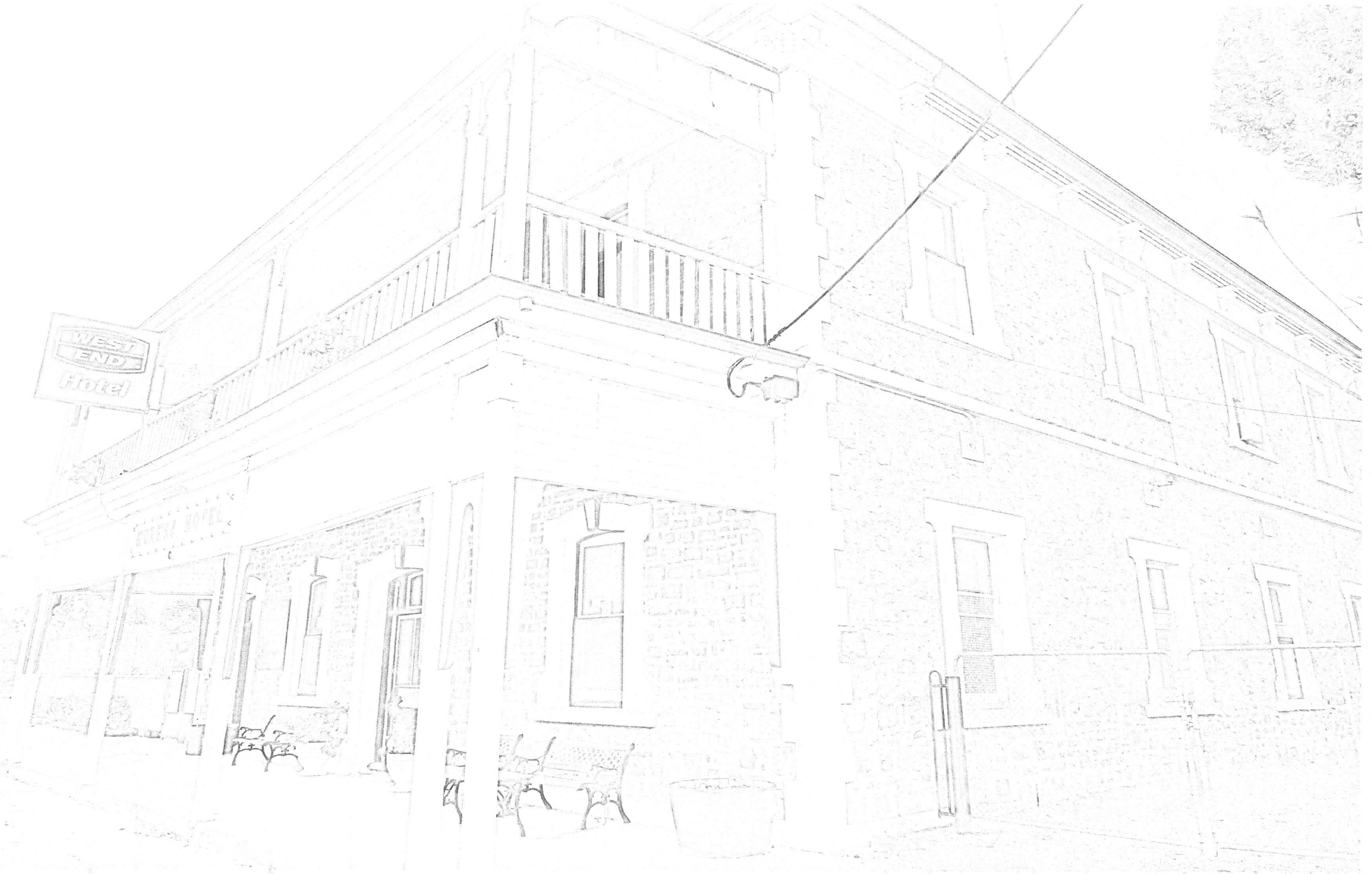
WEST END
Hotel

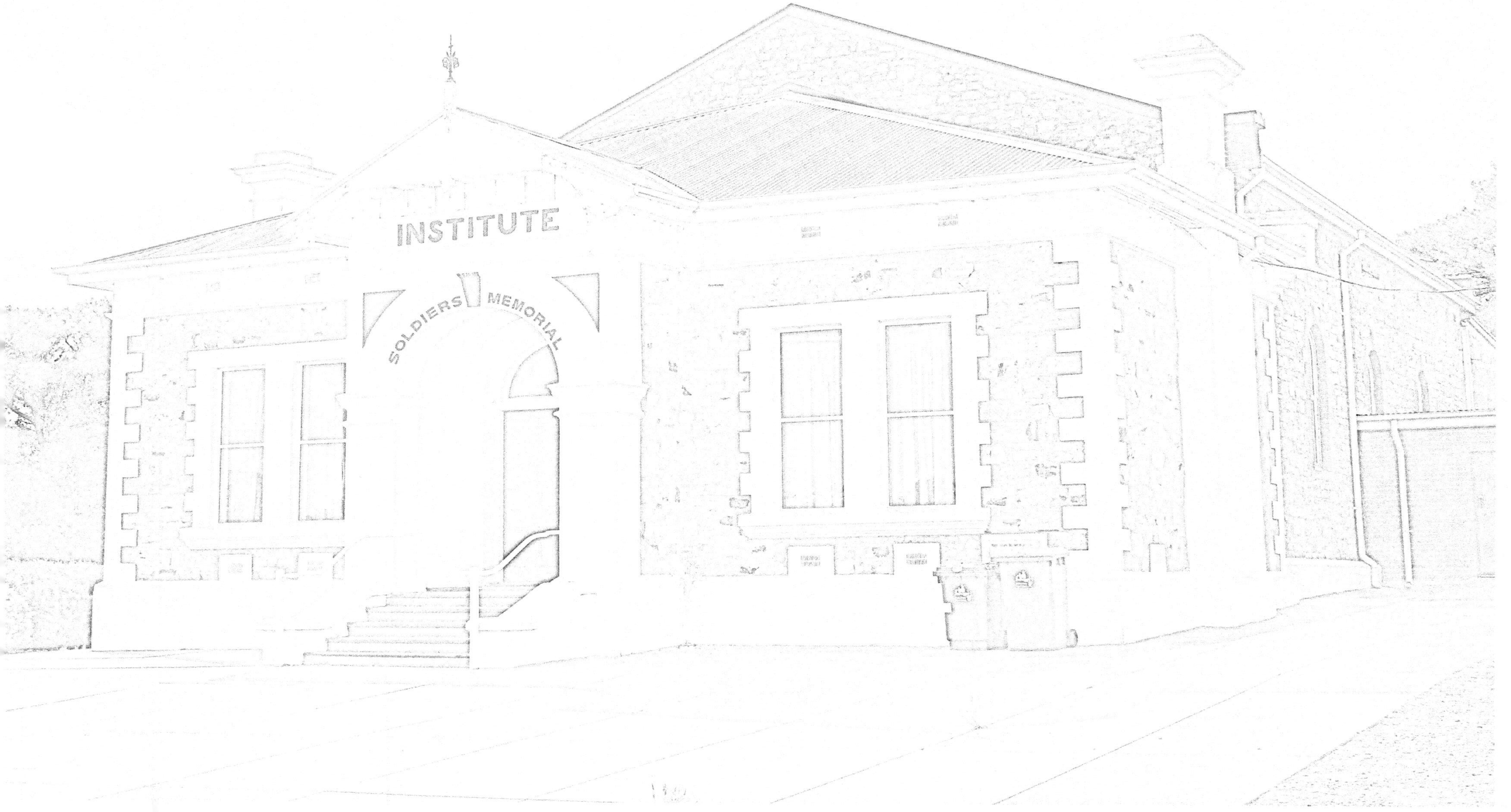
INSTITUTE
SOLDIERS MEMORIAL

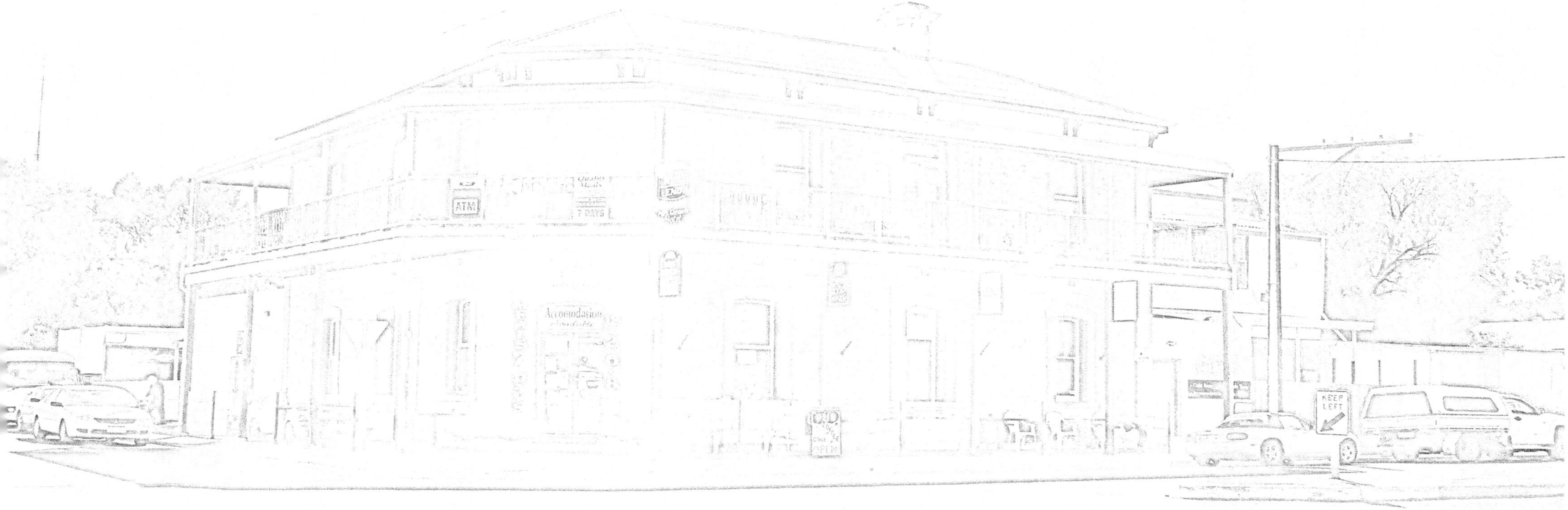
ATM
7 DAYS
Accommodation
KEEP LEFT
OPEN

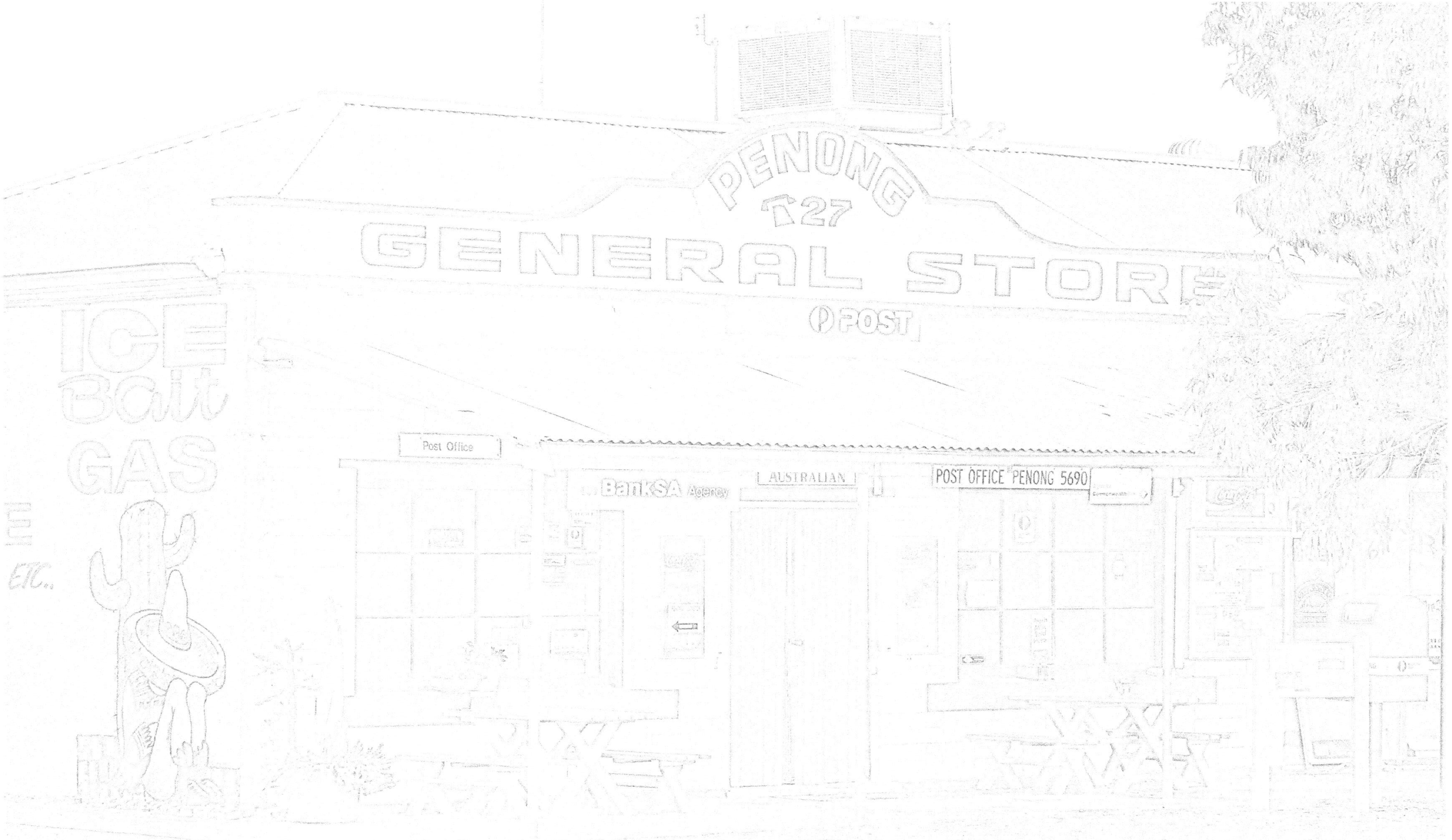
PENONG
27
GENERAL STORE
POST
ICE
Bait
GAS
ETC..
Post Office
BankSA Agency
AUSTRALIAN
POST OFFICE PENONG 5690

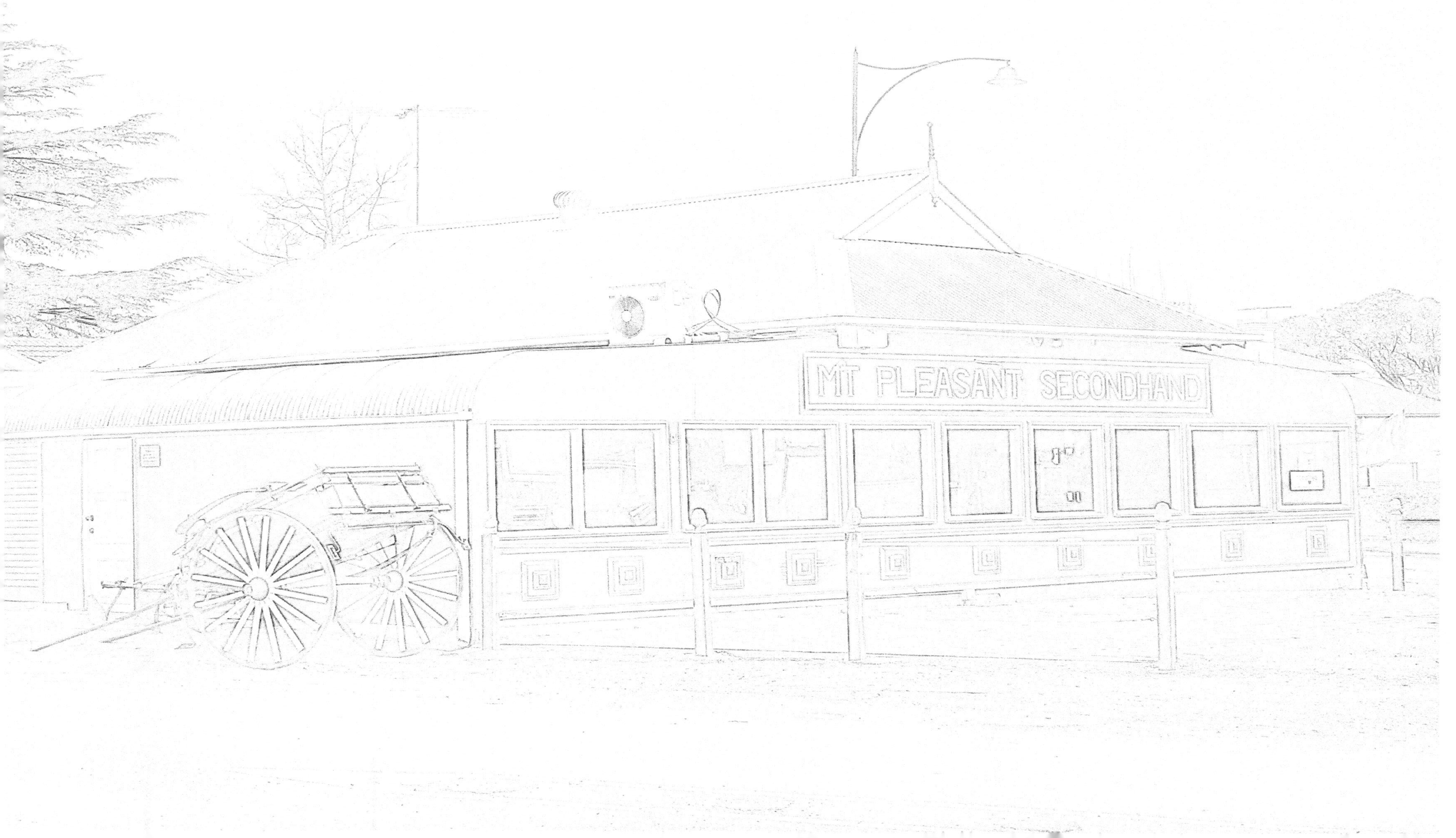
MT PLEASANT SECONDHAND

Dining
&
Gaming

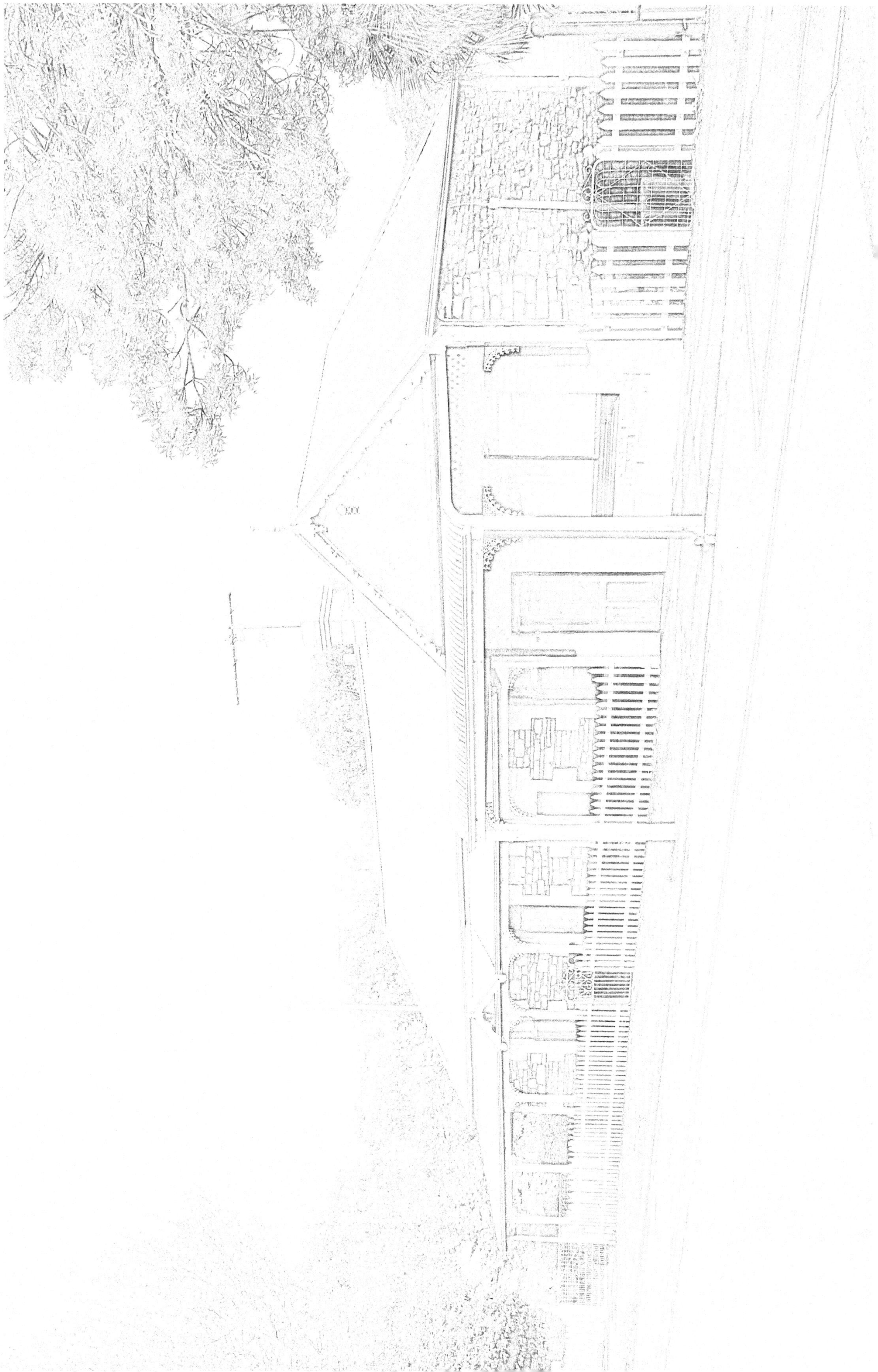

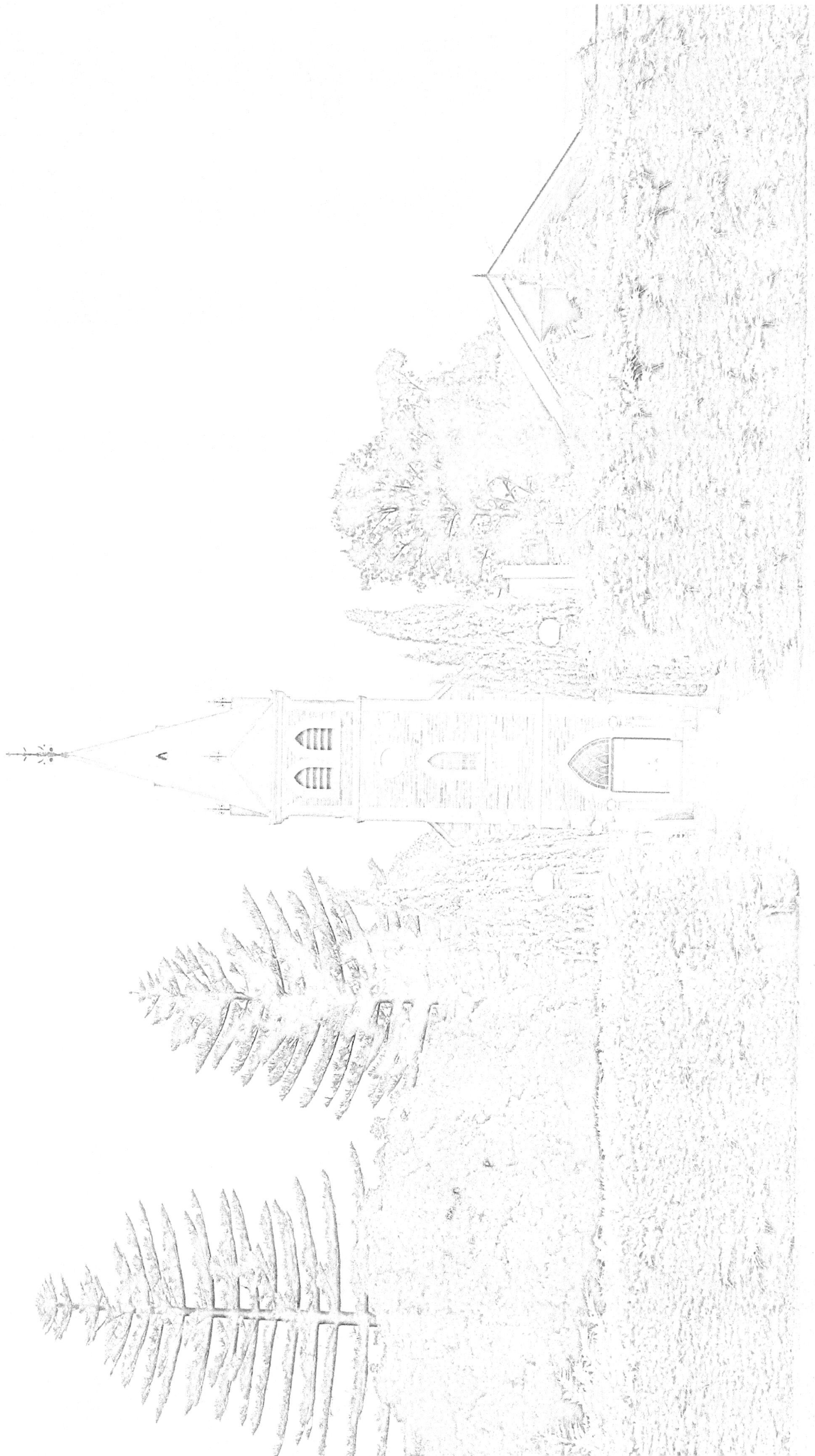

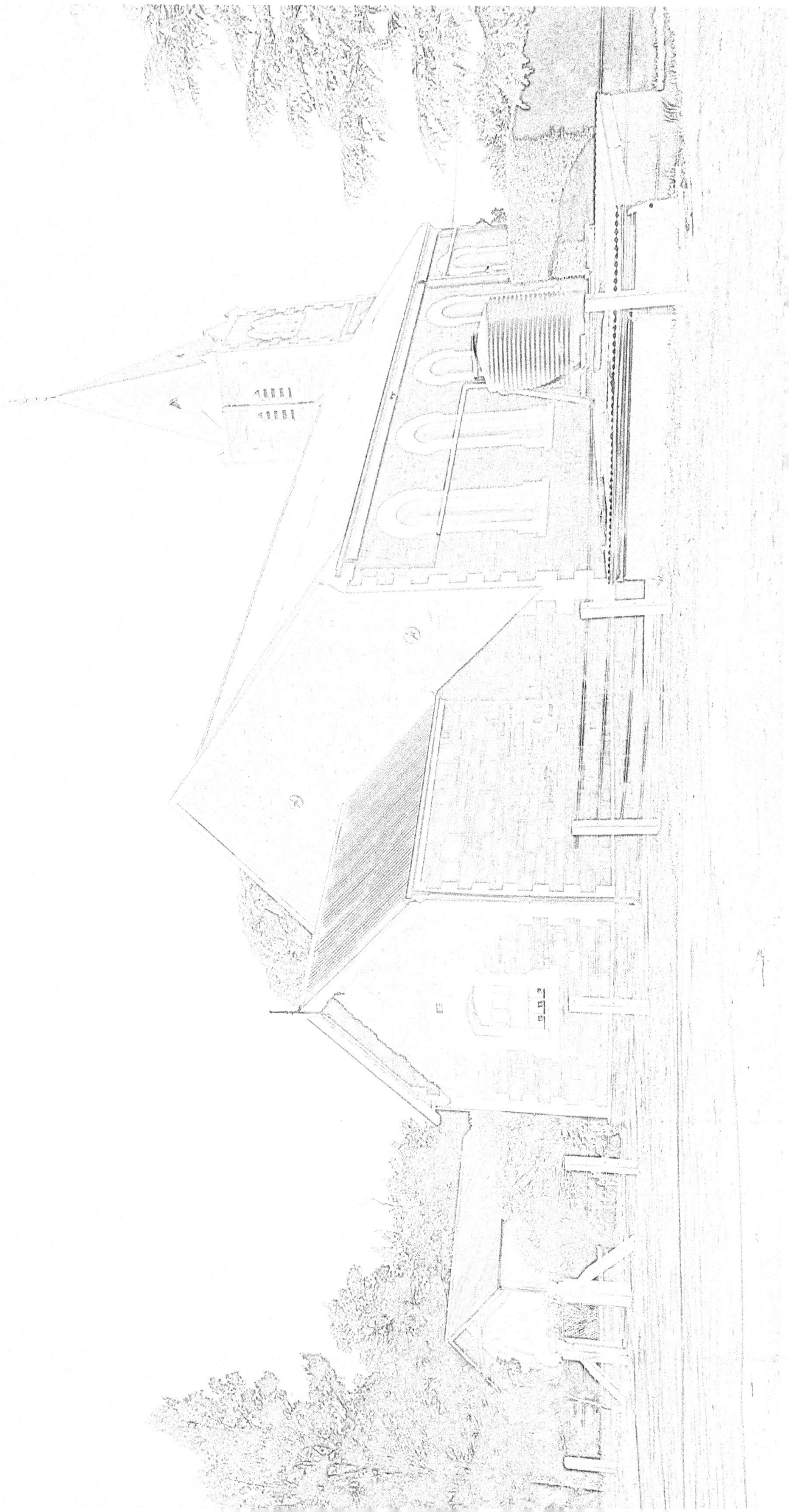

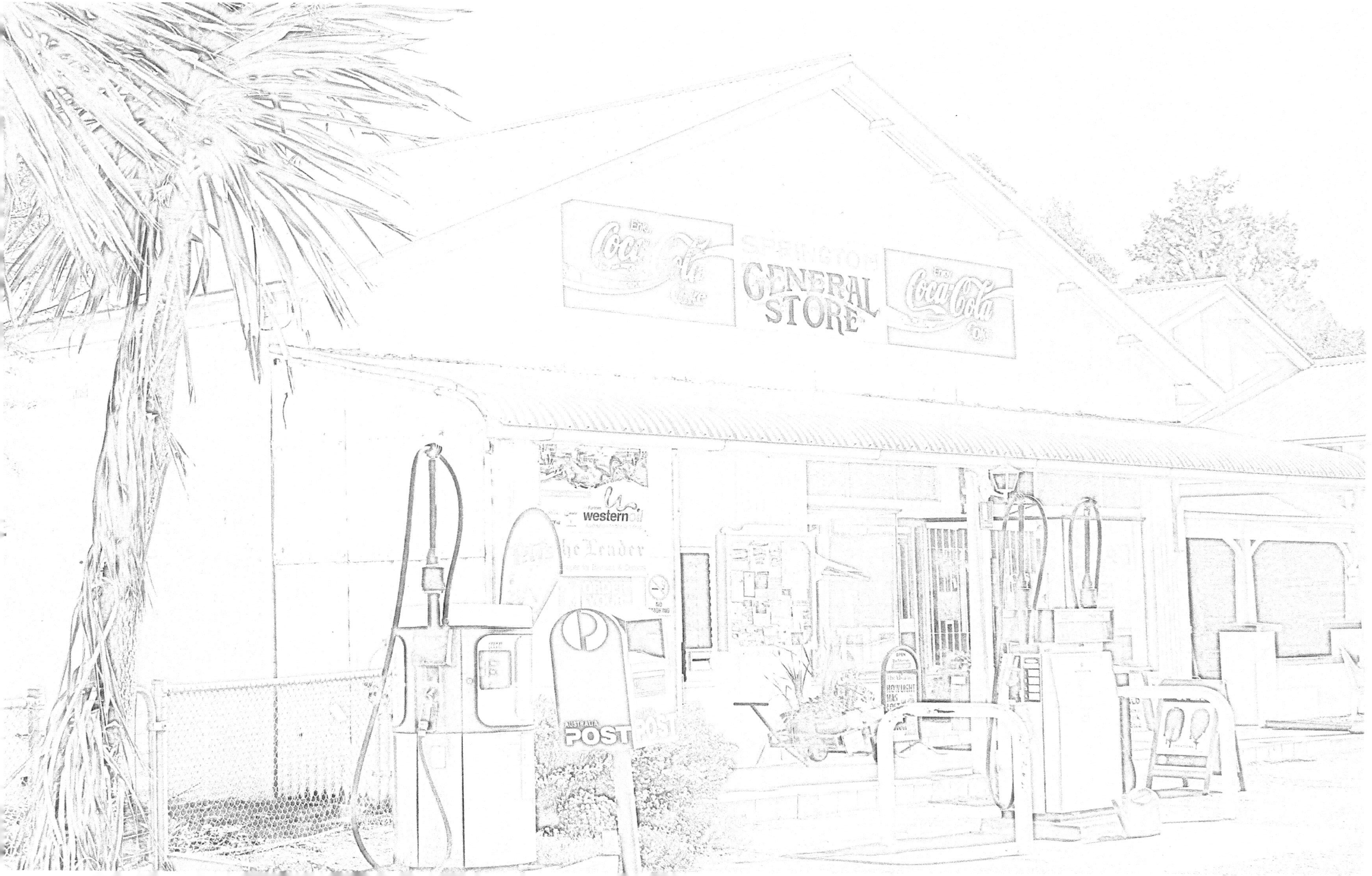
GENERAL STORE
Coca-Cola
Coca-Cola
westernoil
NO SMOKING
POST

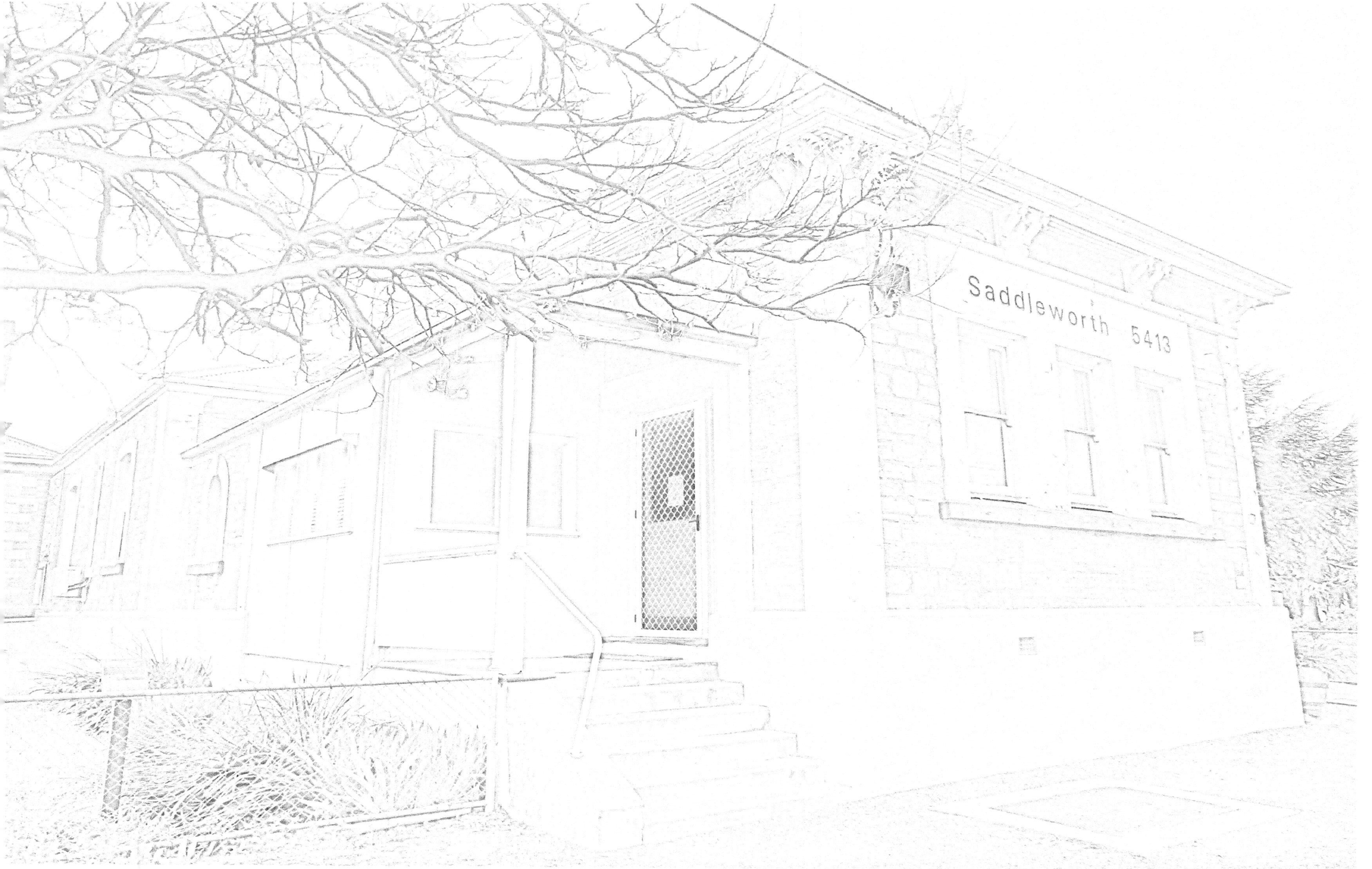
Saddleworth 5413

POST
POST OFFICE
POST

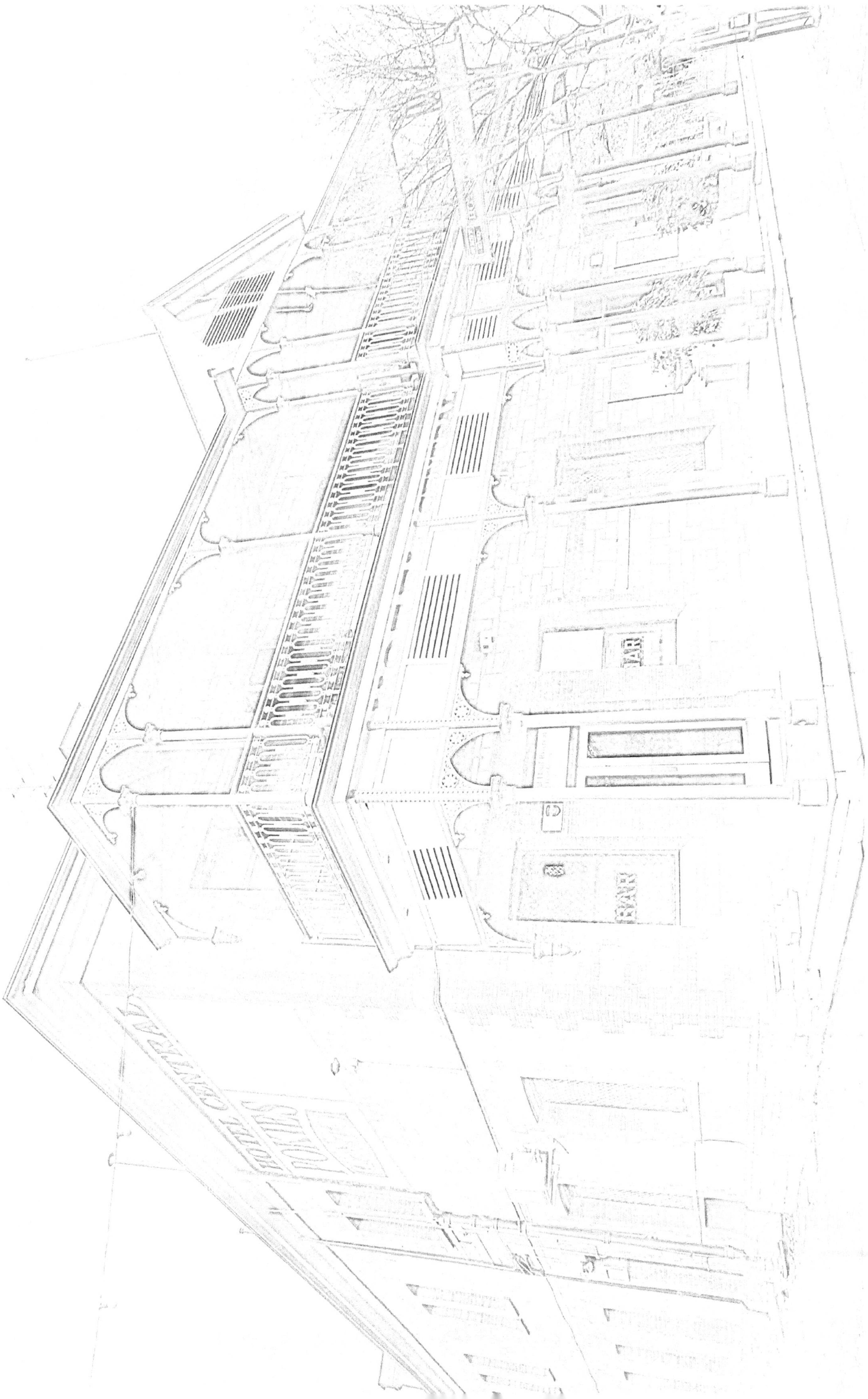
HOTEL CENTRAL
POKIES
BAR
BAR

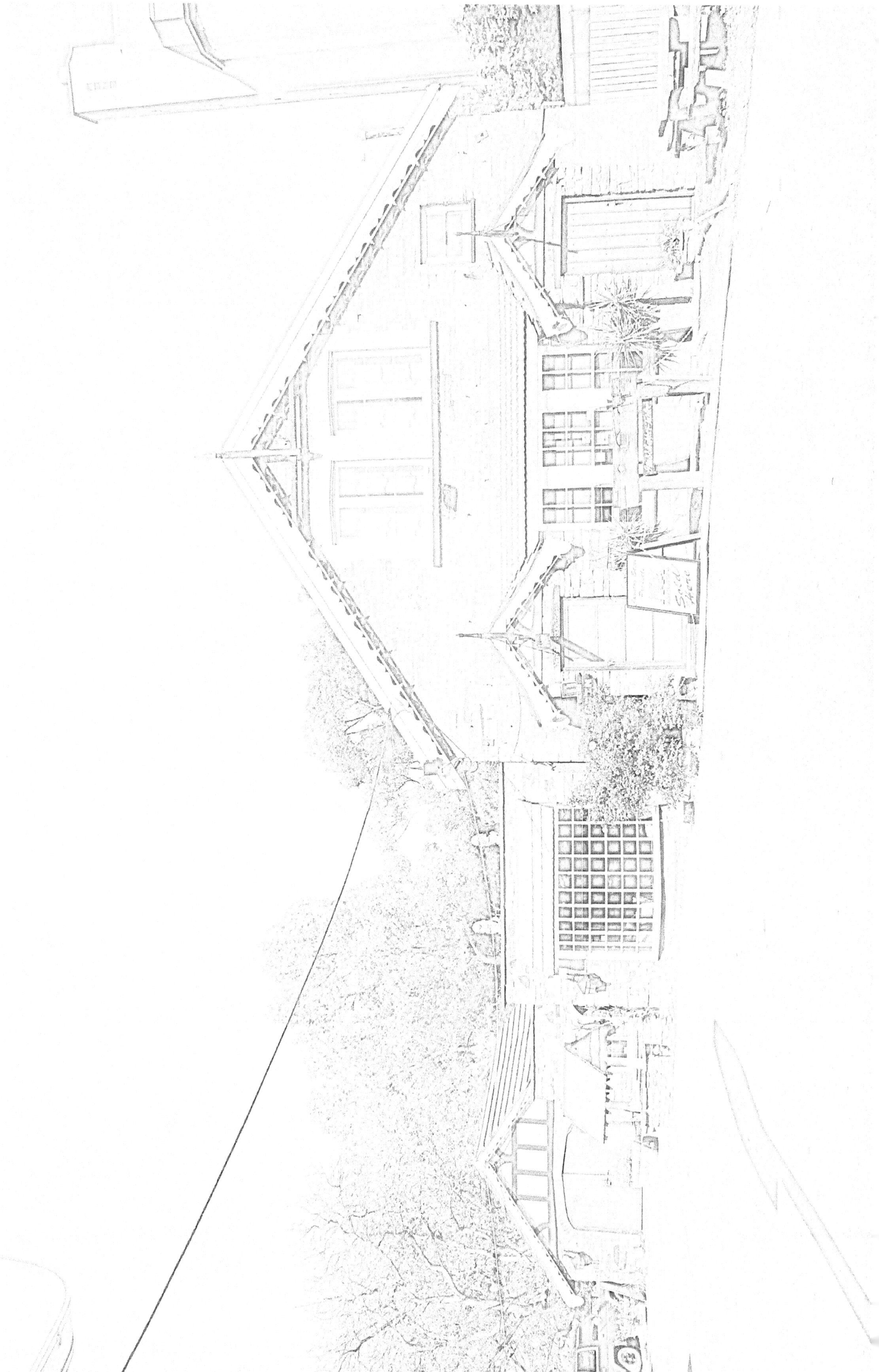

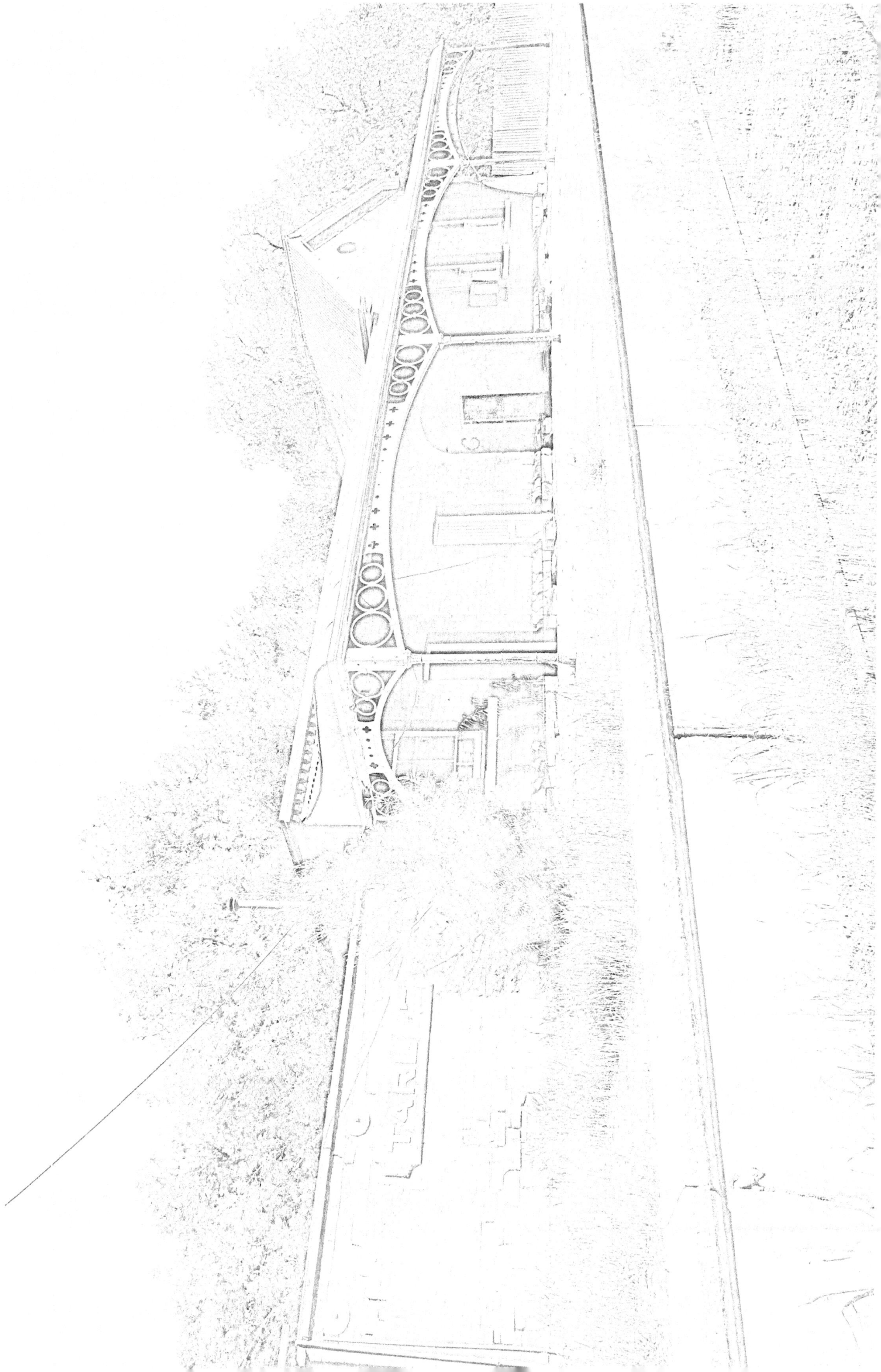

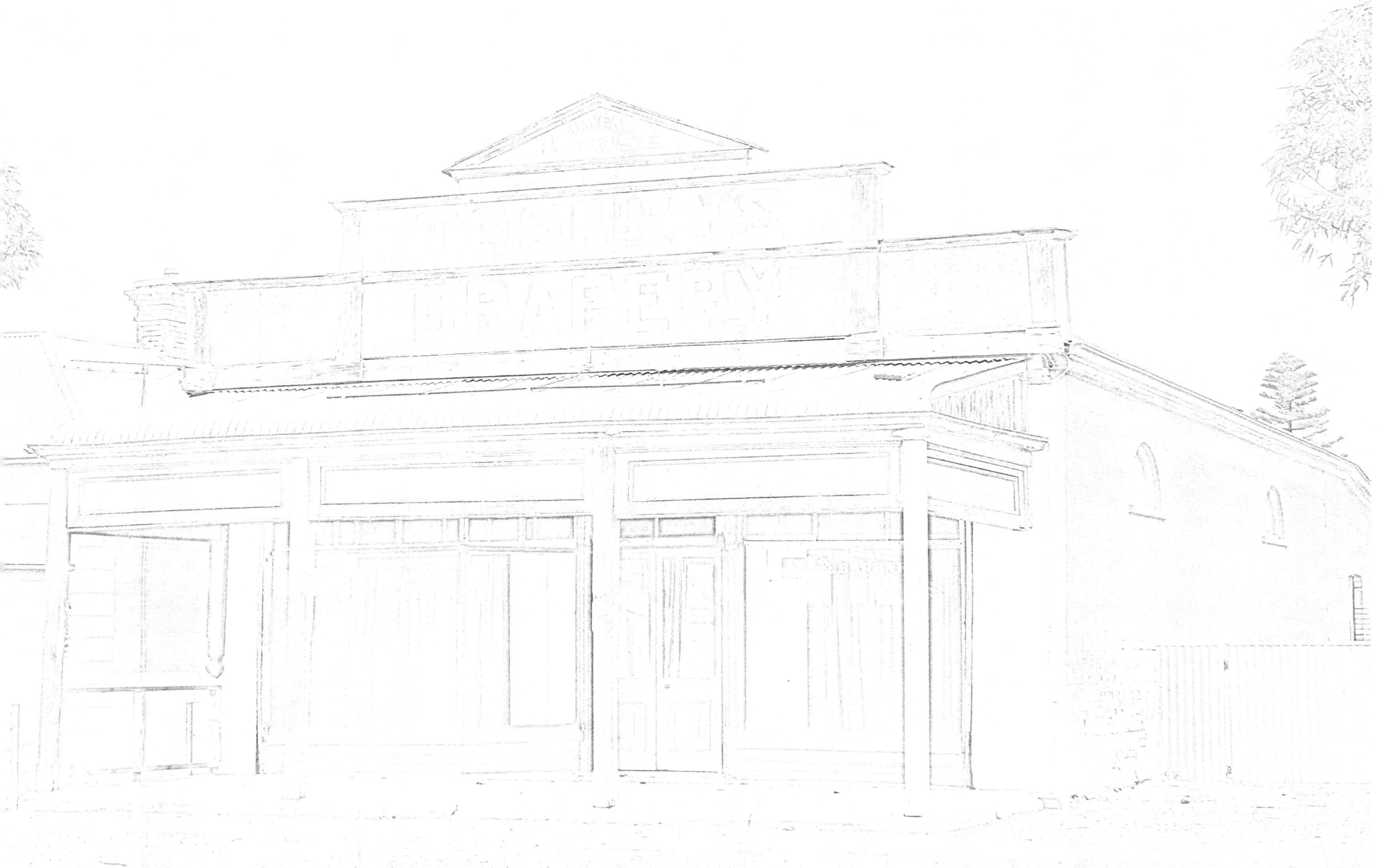
DRAPERY

THE GRAIN STORE
Hooker

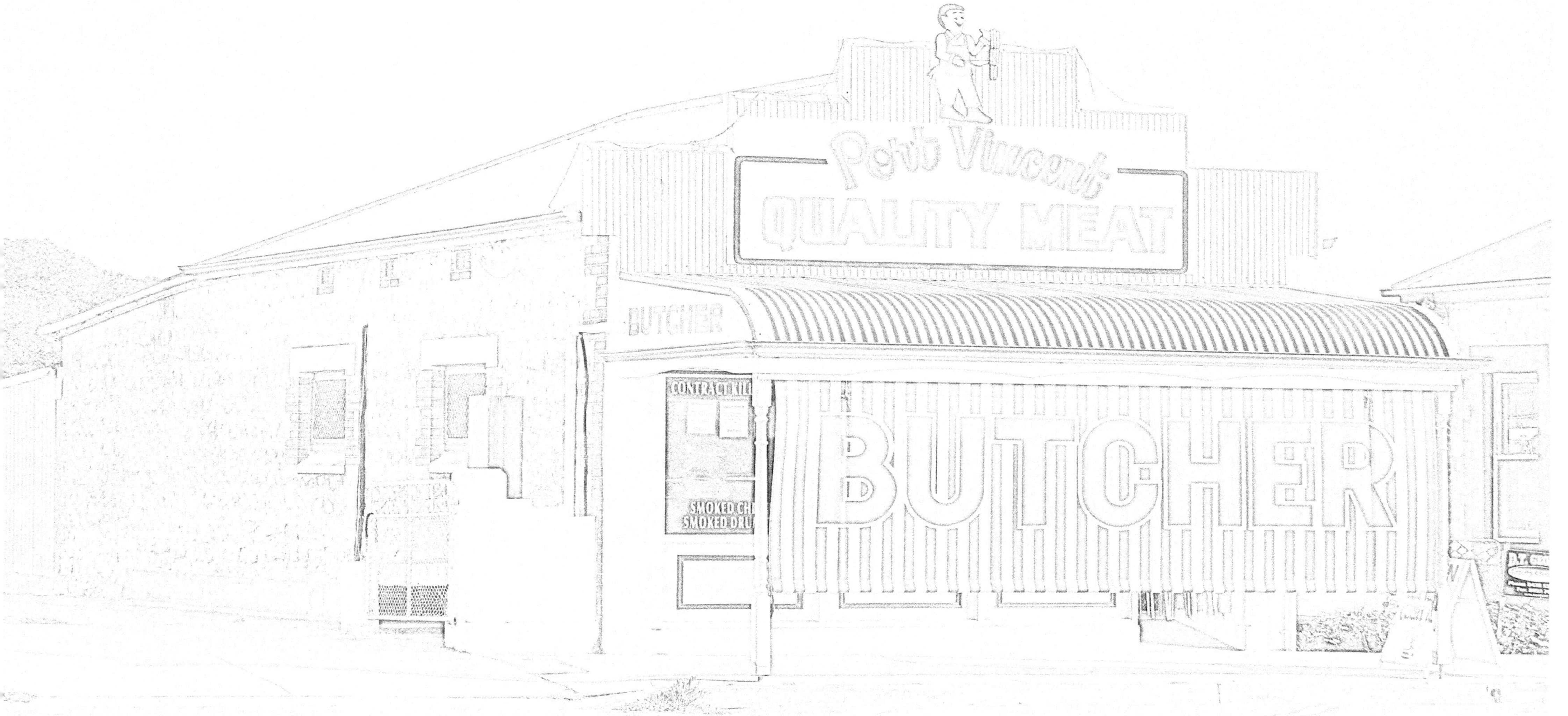
Port Vincent
QUALITY MEAT
BUTCHER
BUTCHER

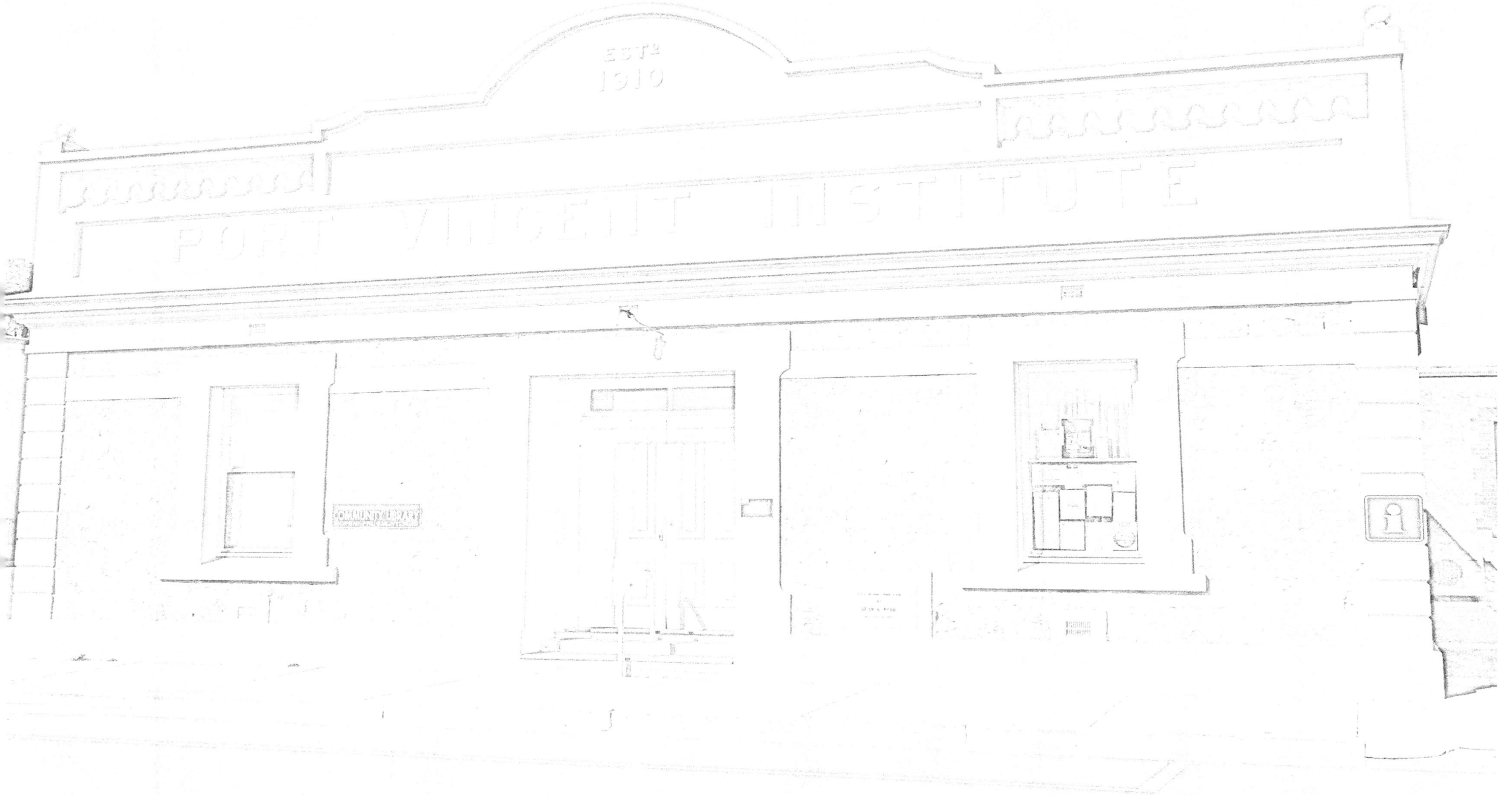
ESTD
1919
PORT VINCENT INSTITUTE
COMMUNITY LIBRARY

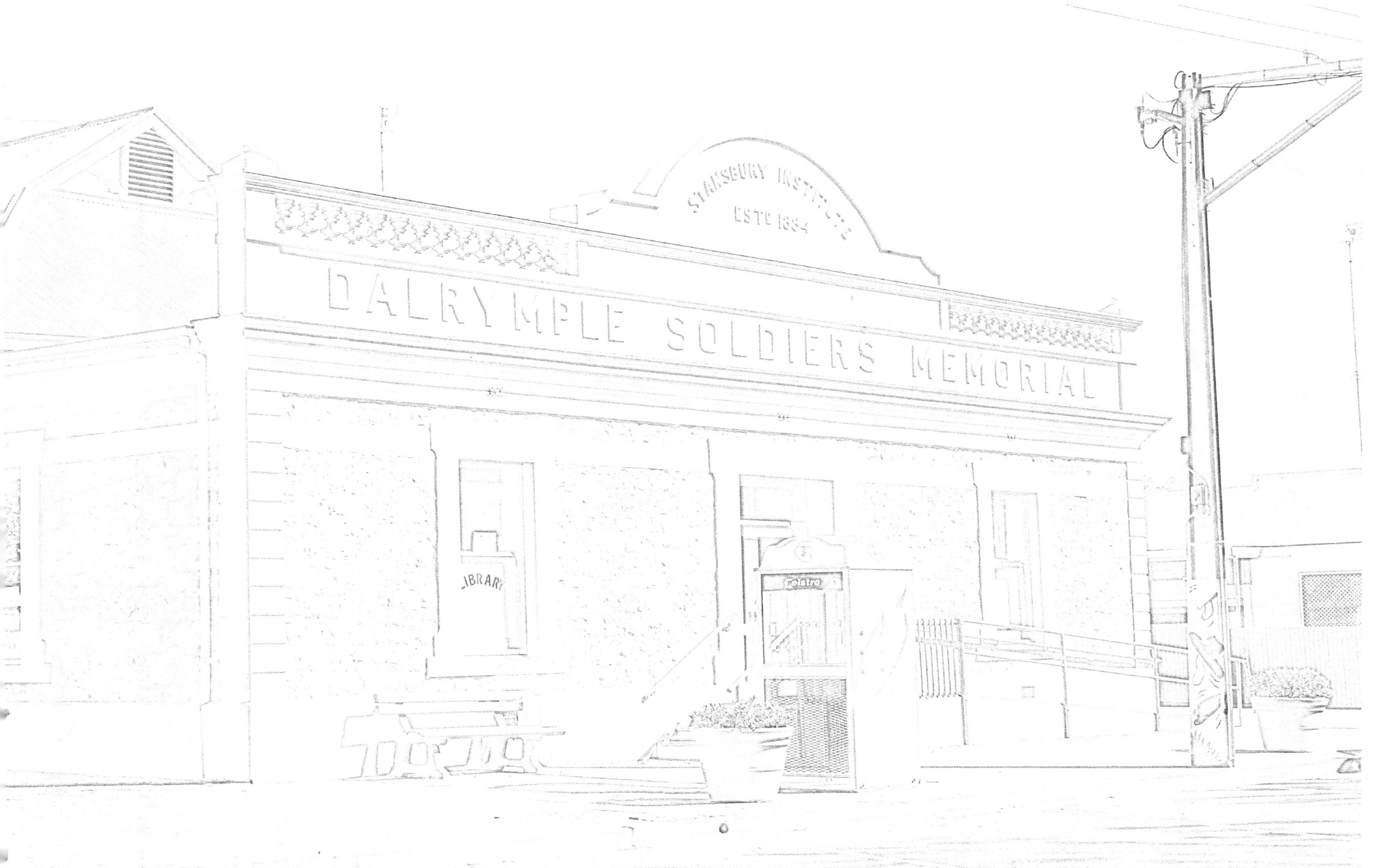
STANSBURY INSTITUTE
ESTD 1884
DALRYMPLE SOLDIERS MEMORIAL
LIBRARY
Telstra

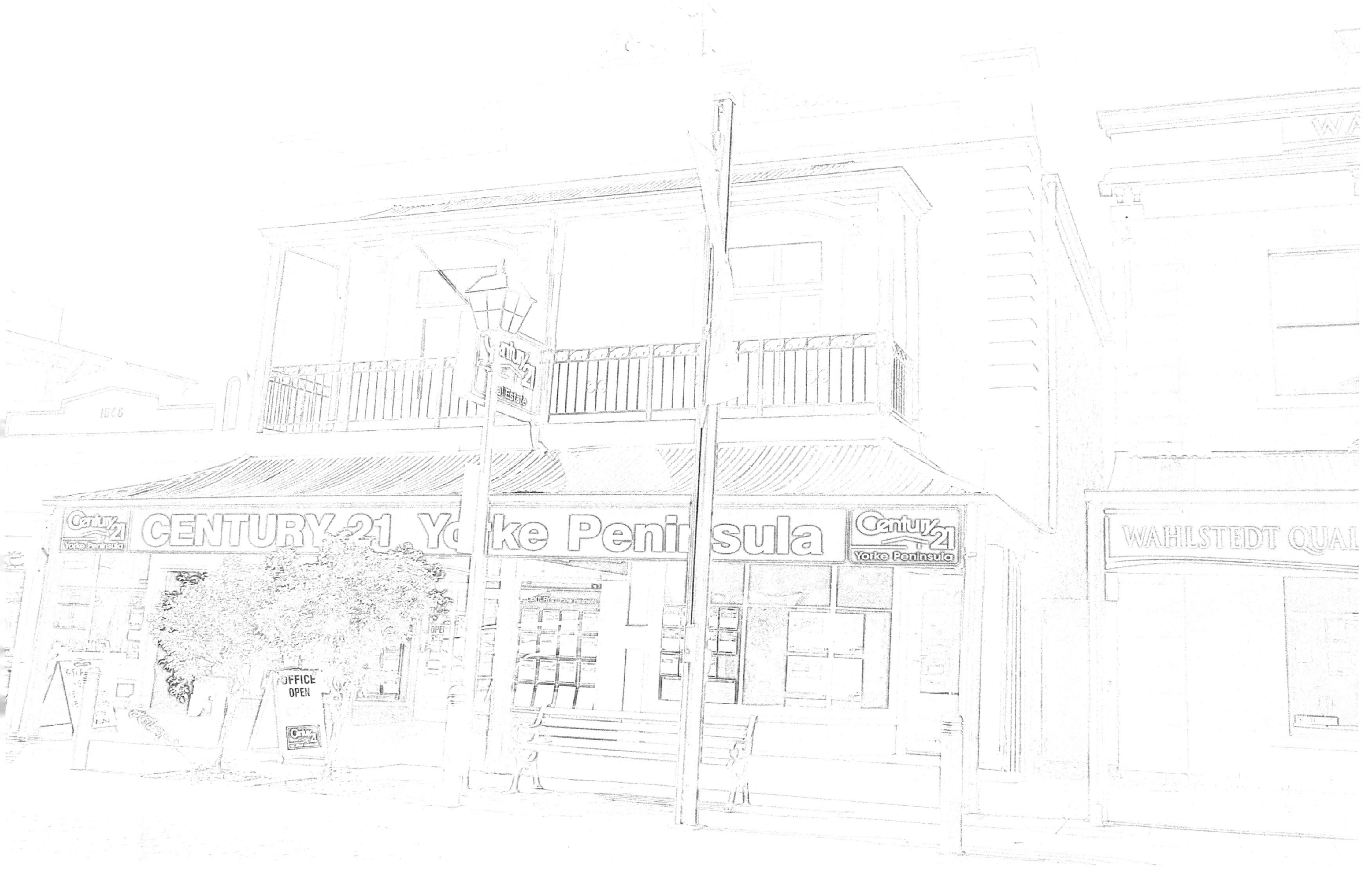
CENTURY 21 Yorke Peninsula
Century 21
Yorke Peninsula
Century 21
Yorke Peninsula
OFFICE
OPEN
WAHLSTEDT QUAL

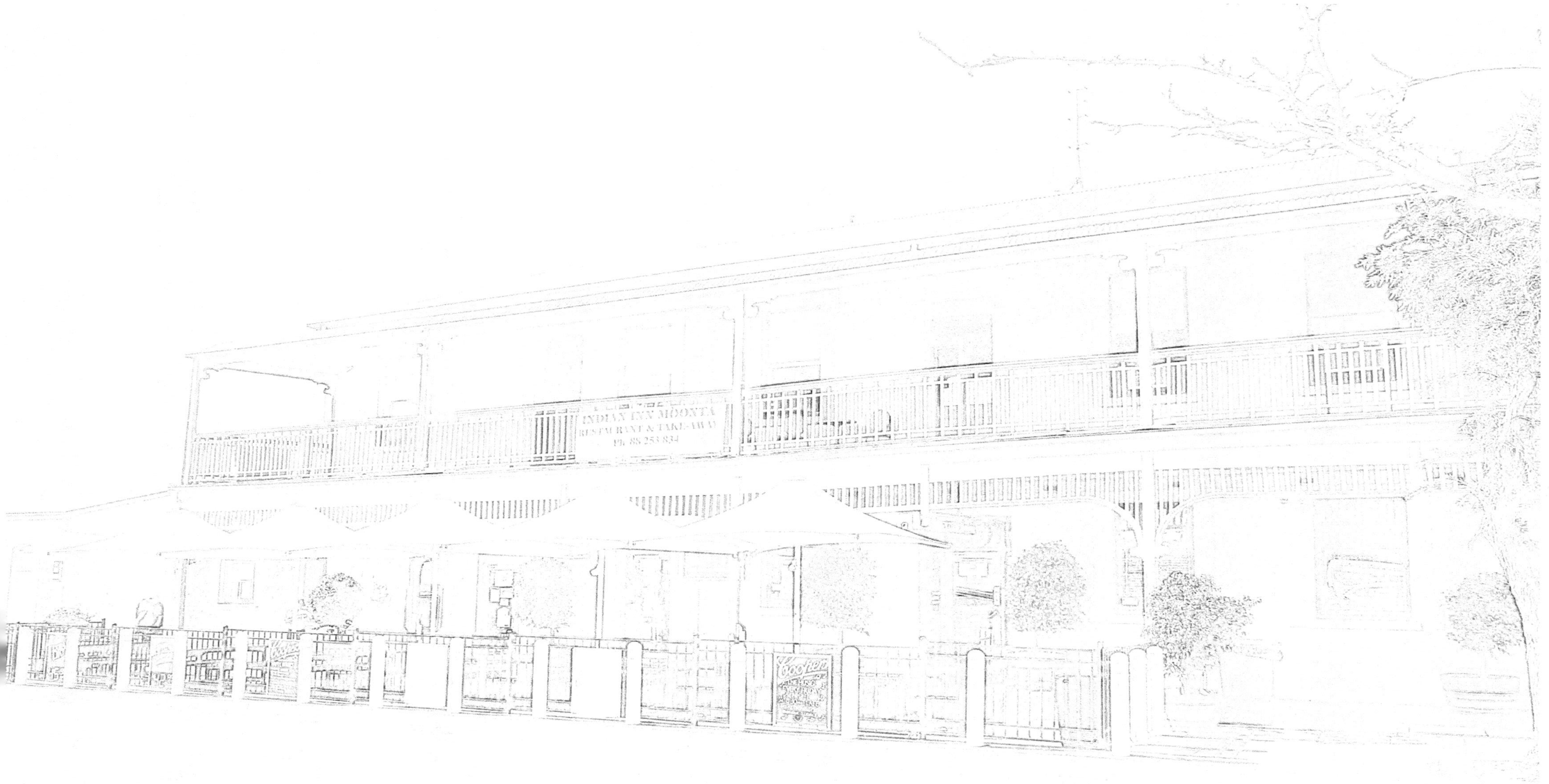
INDIAN INN MOONTA
RESTAURANT & TAKE-AWAY
Ph 88 253 834
Coopers

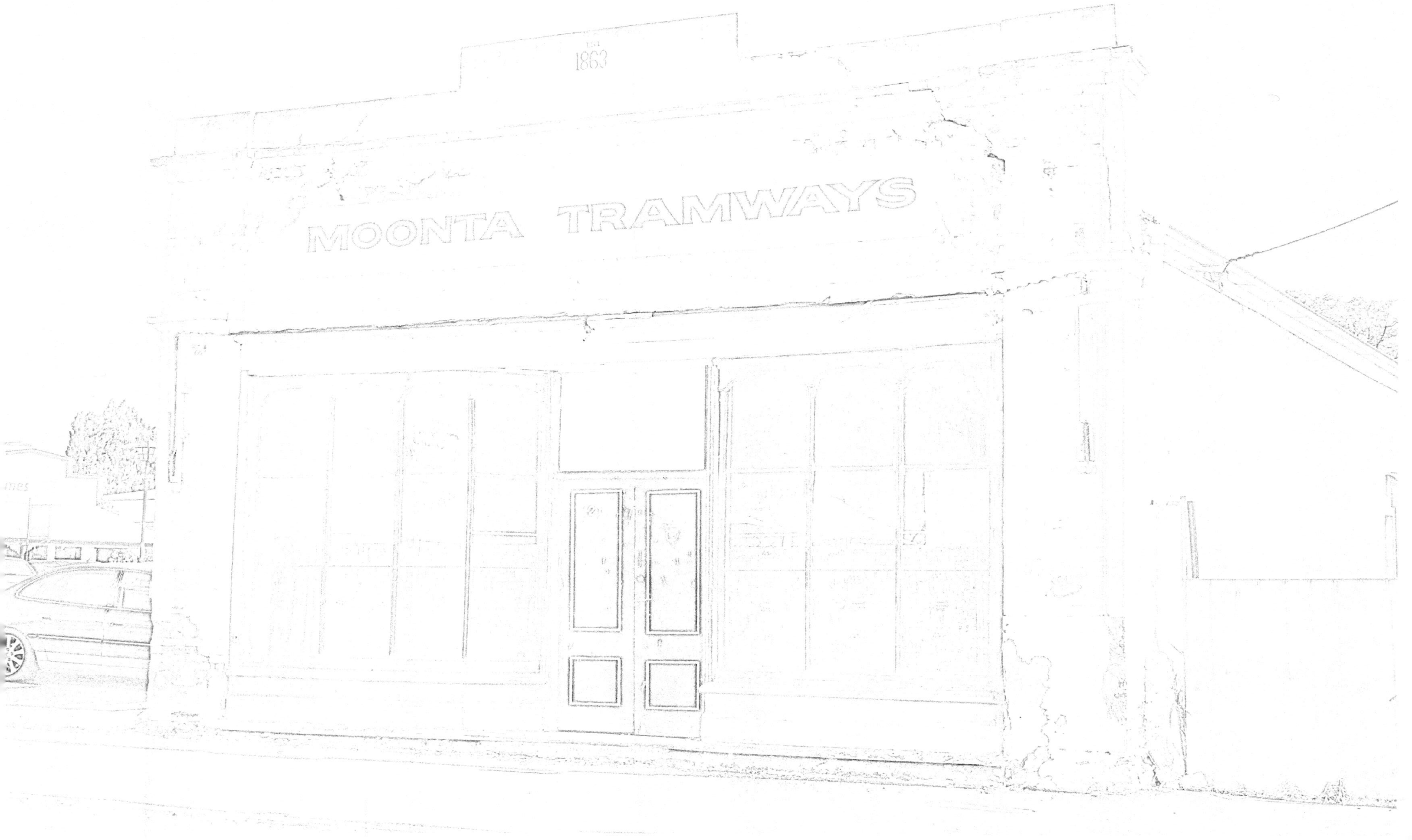
EST
1863
MOONTA TRAMWAYS

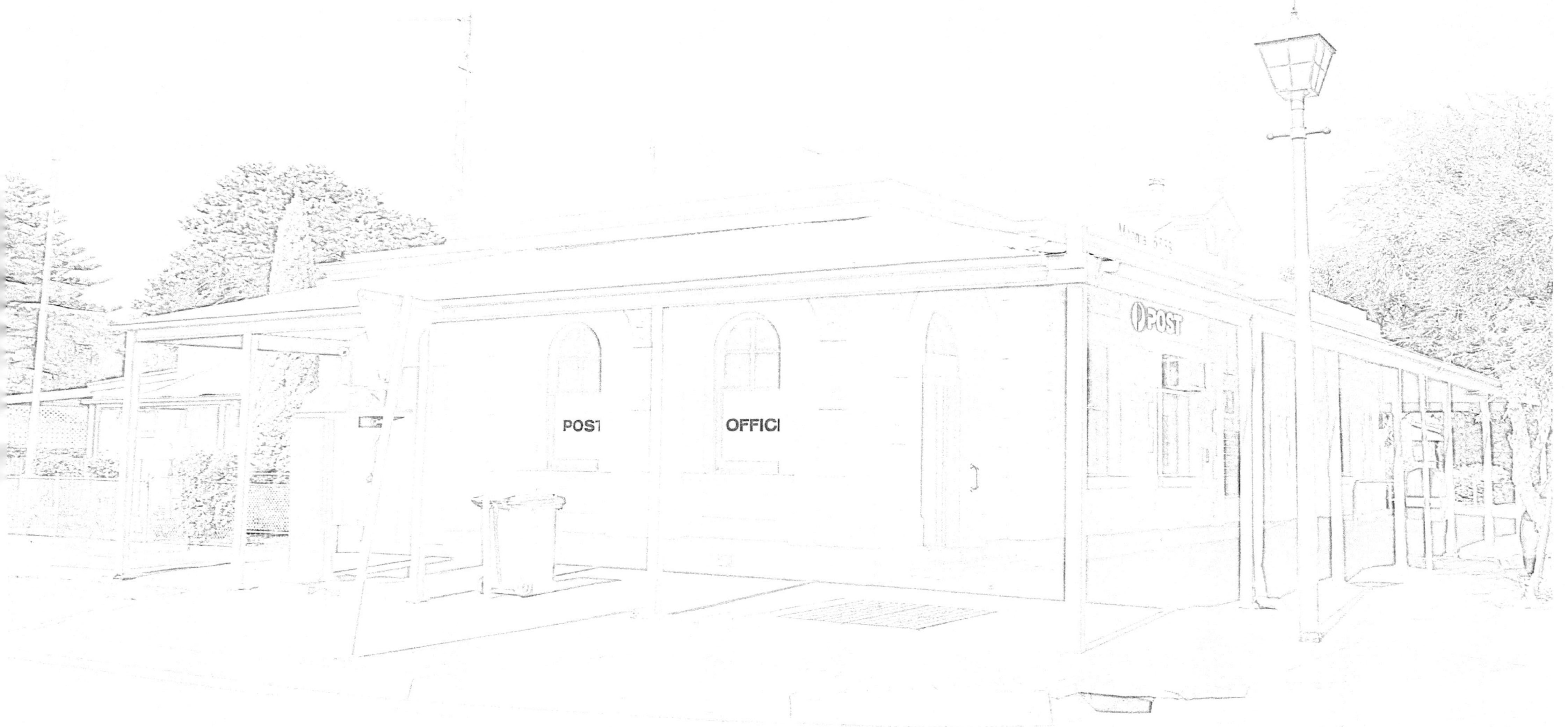
POST
OFFICI
POST

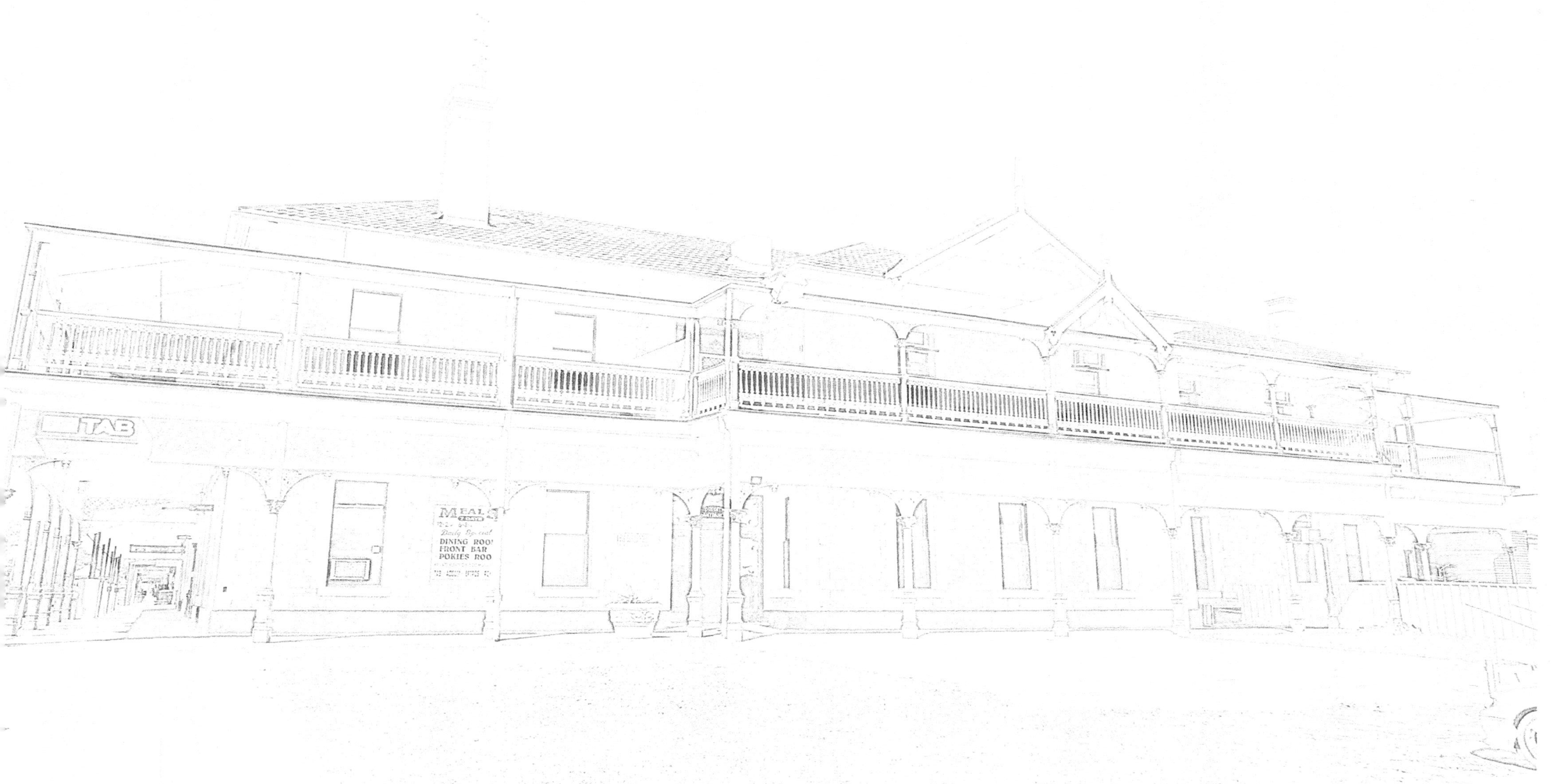
TAB
MEALS
Daily Special
DINING ROO
FRONT BAR
POKIES ROO

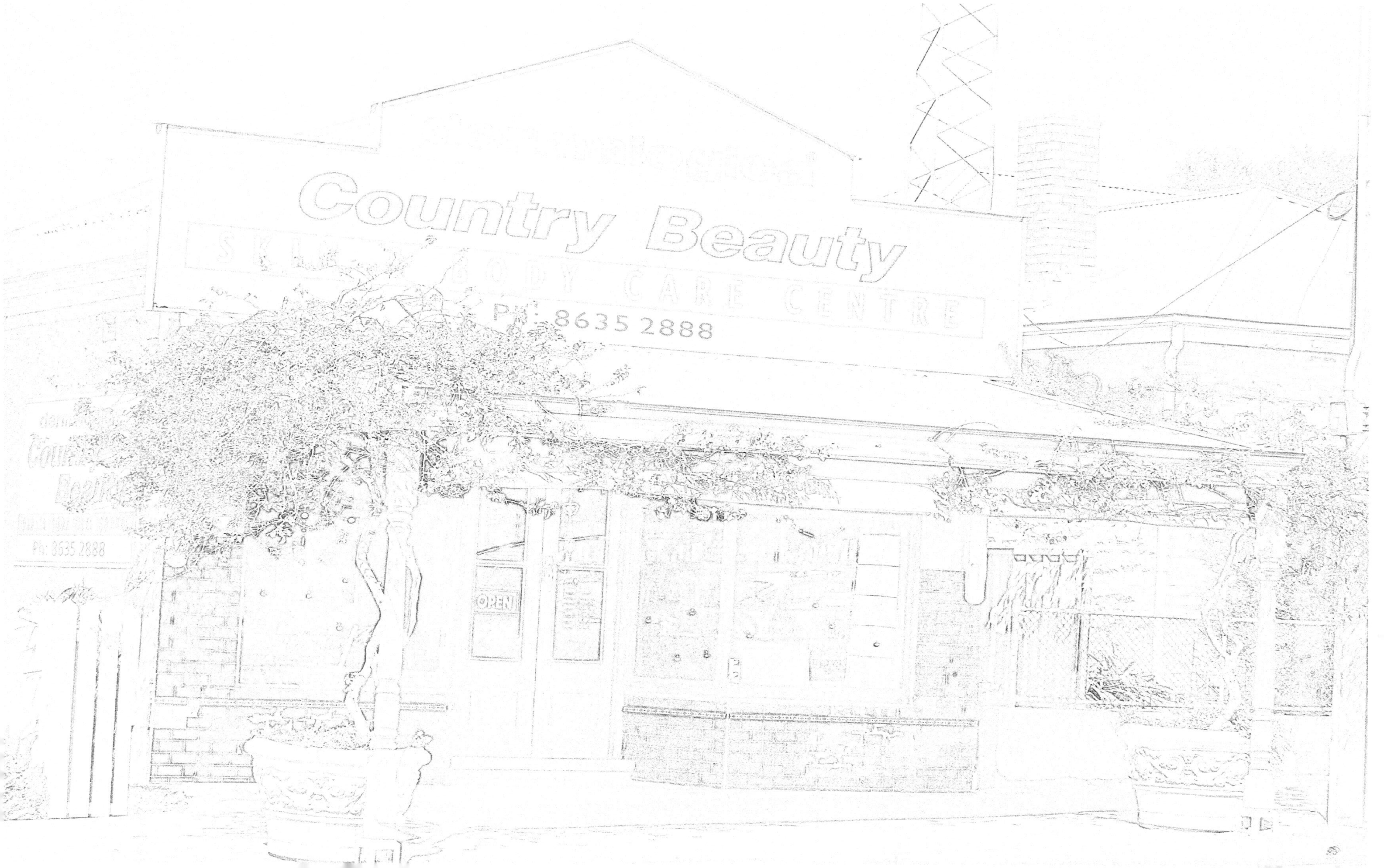
Country Beauty
SKIN BODY CARE CENTRE
Ph: 8635 2888
OPEN
Ph: 8635 2888

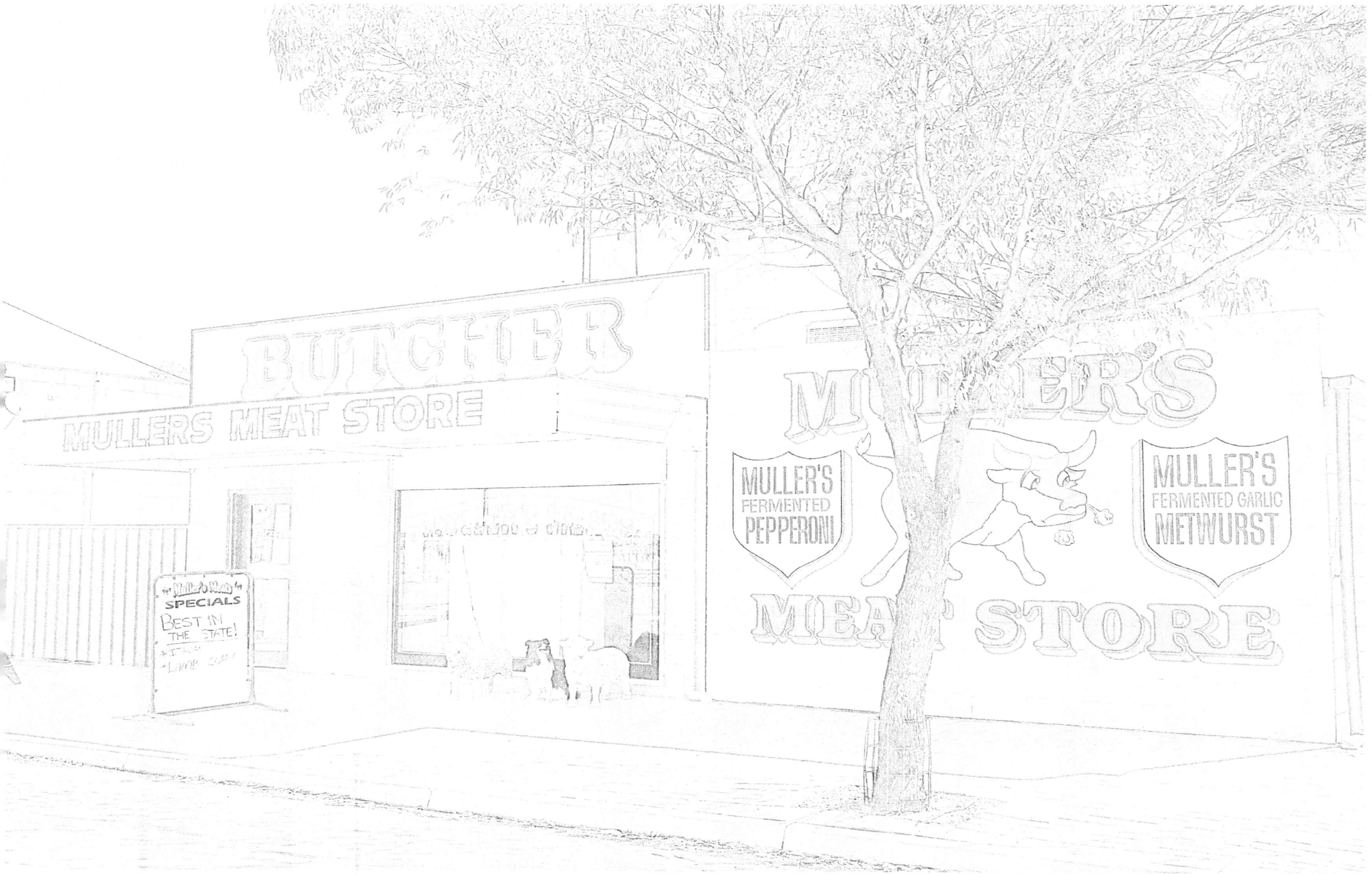
BUTCHER
MULLERS MEAT STORE
MULLER'S
MEAT STORE
MULLER'S
FERMENTED
PEPPERONI
MULLER'S
FERMENTED GARLIC
METWURST
SPECIALS
BEST IN
THE STATE!

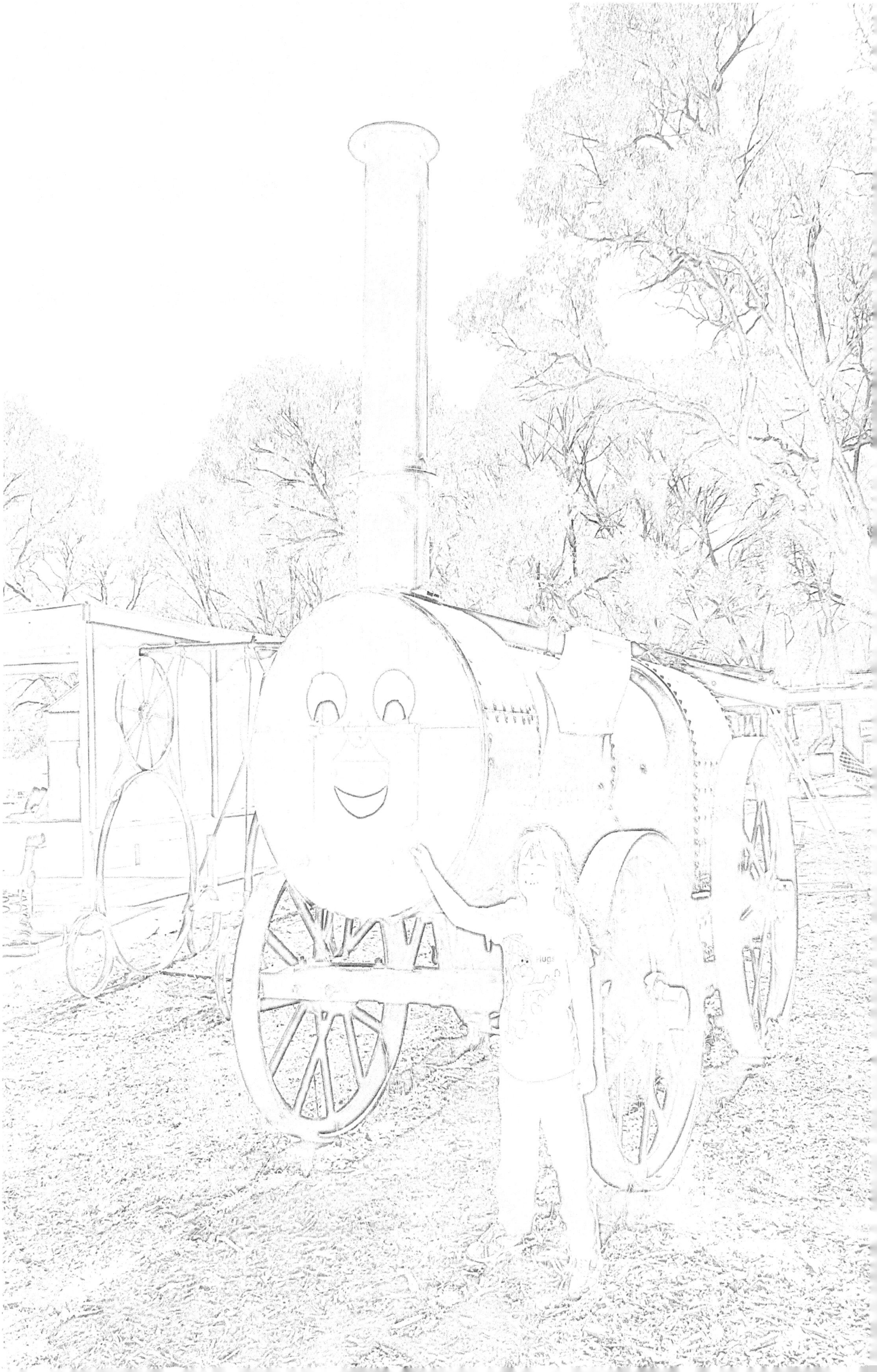

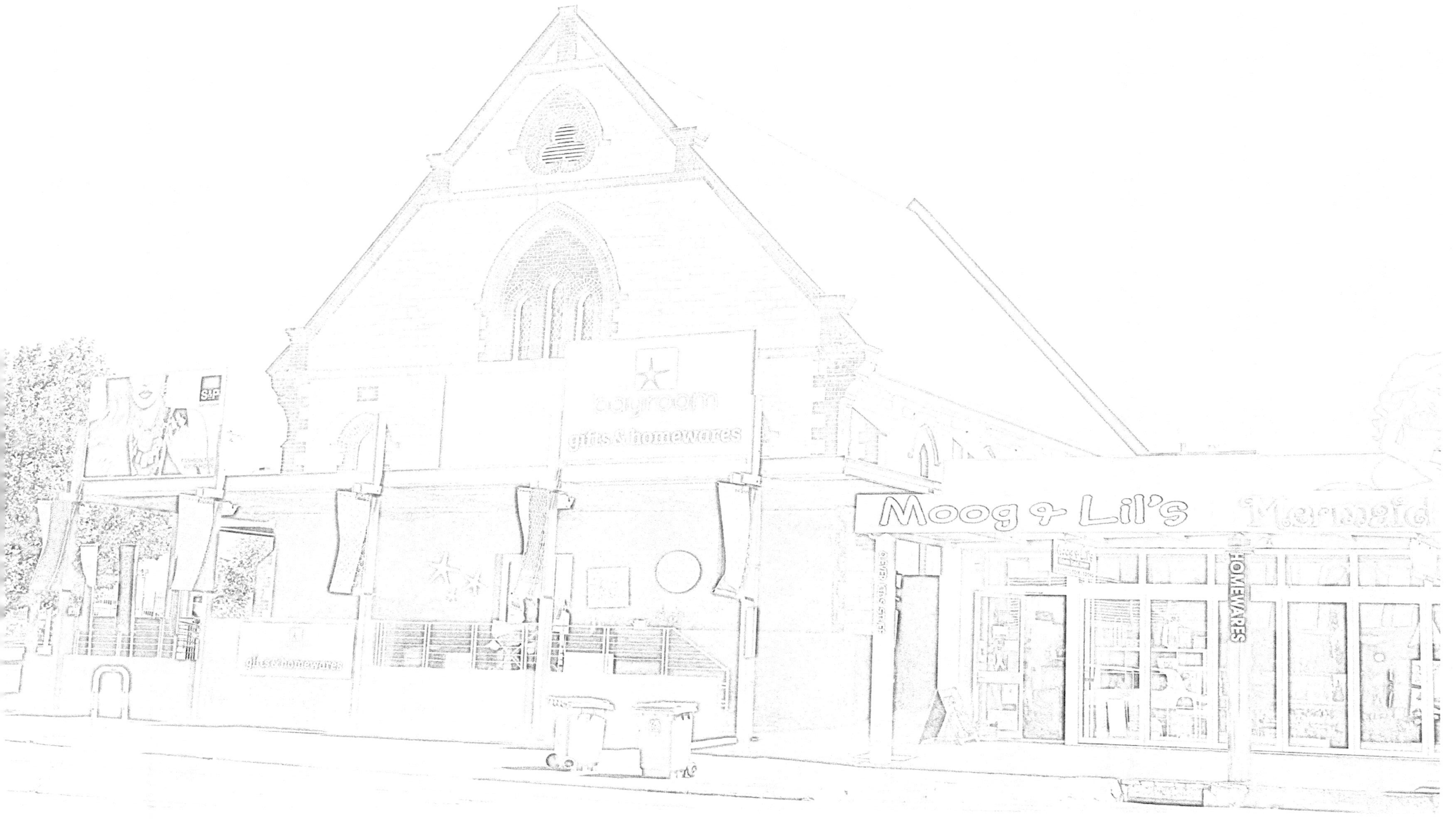

Moog & Lil's
HOMEWARES
gifts & homewares

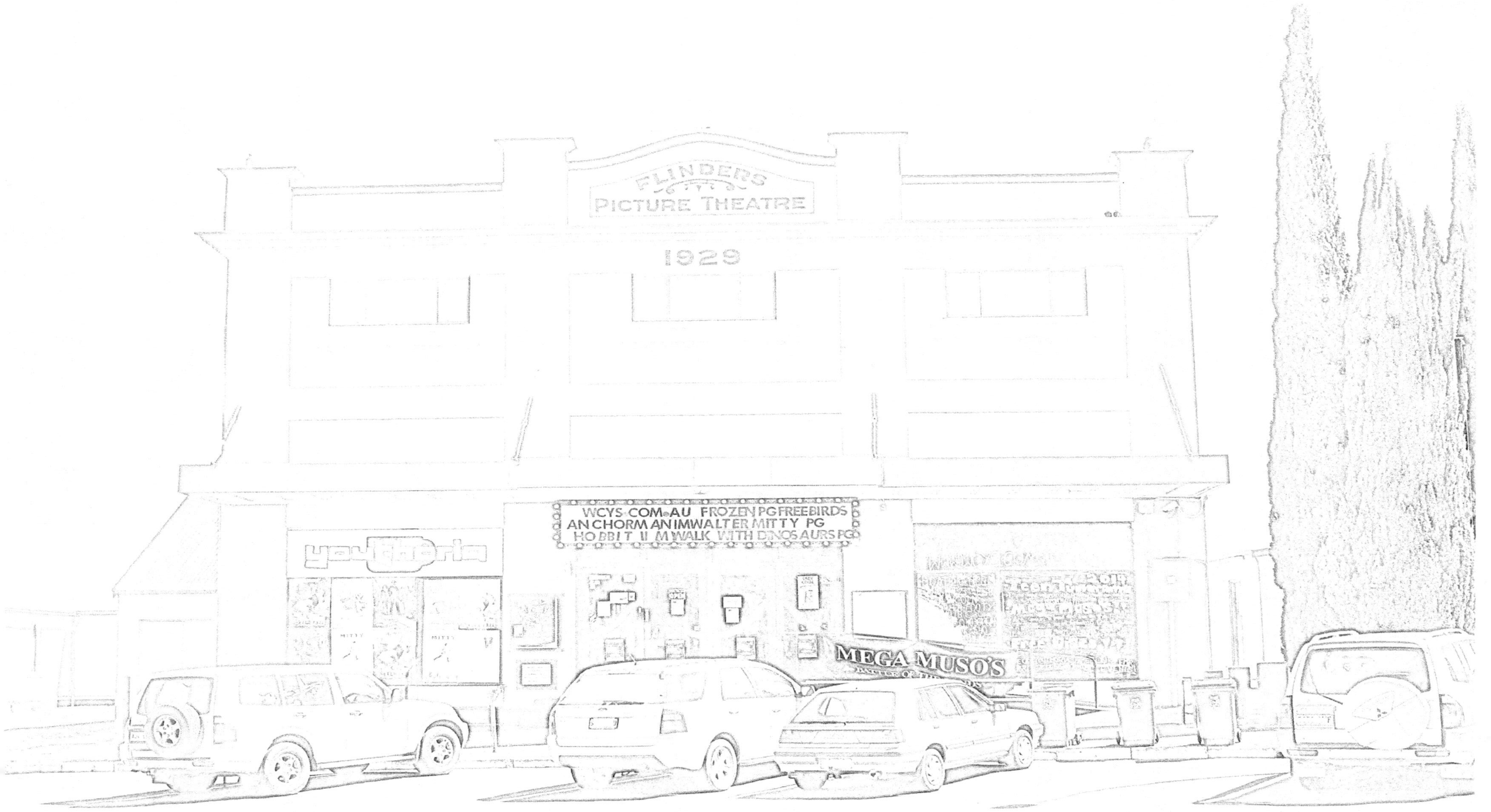
FLINDERS
PICTURE THEATRE
1929
WCYS.COM.AU FROZEN PG FREEBIRDS
ANCHORMAN IMWALTER MITTY PG
HOBBIT II MWALK WITH DINOSAURS PG
MEGA MUSO'S

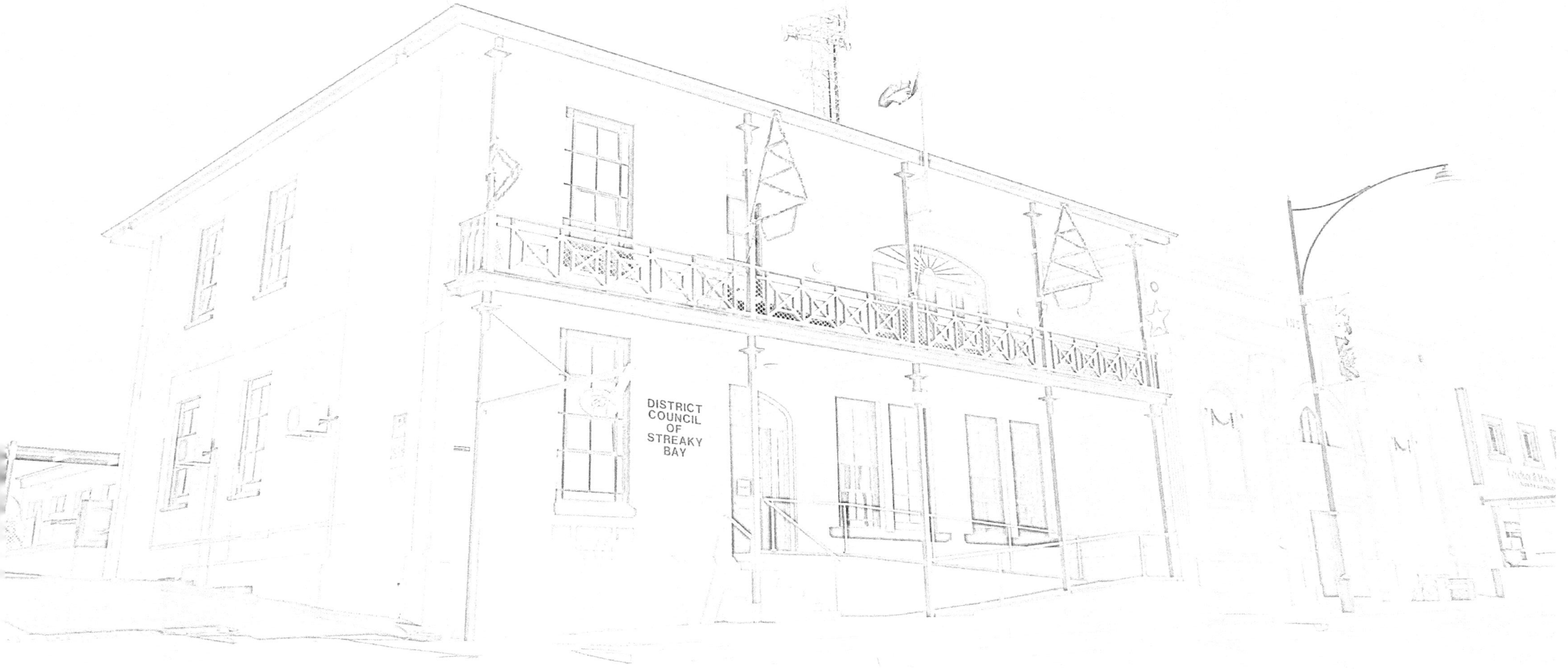
DISTRICT
COUNCIL
OF
STREAKY
BAY

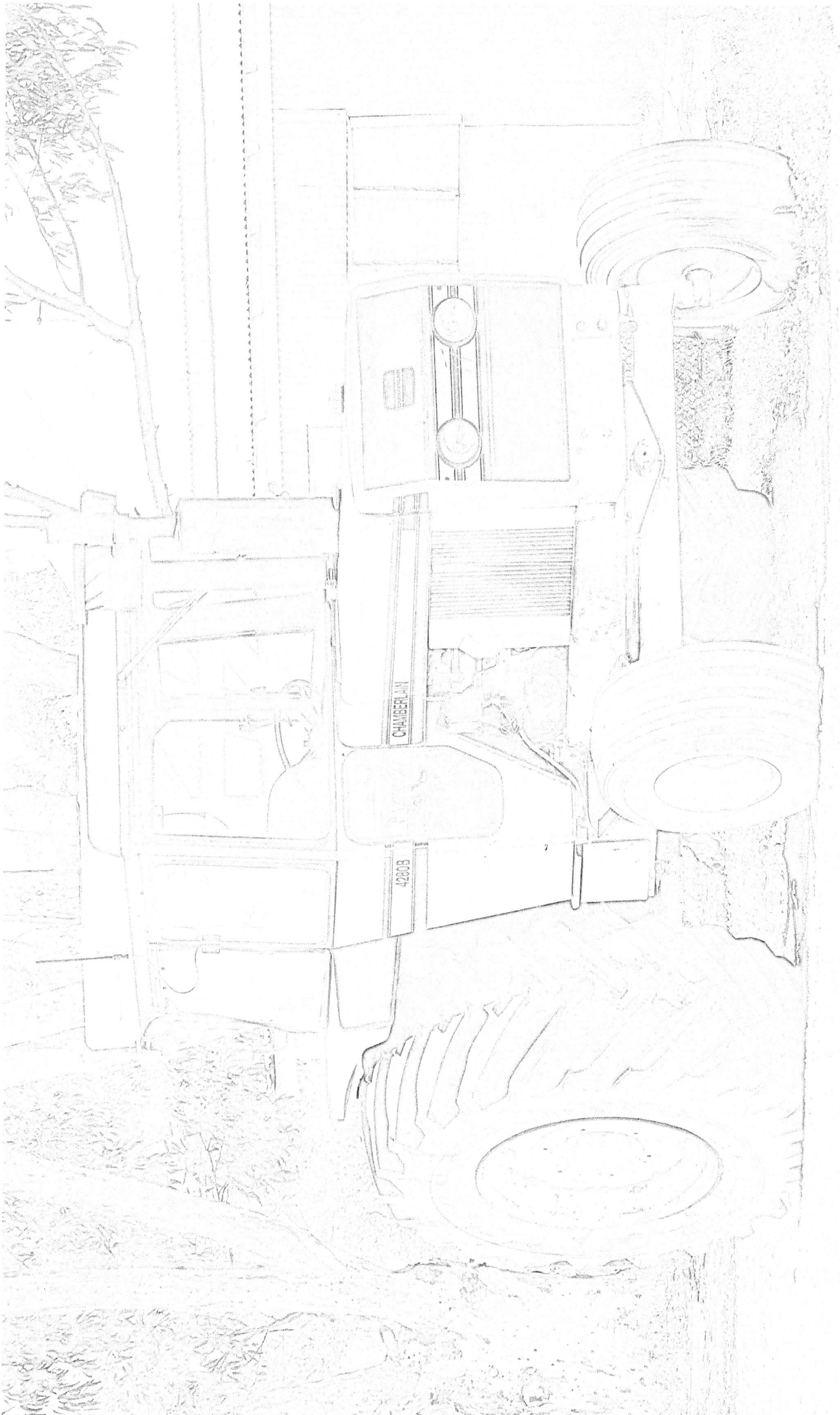
CHAMBERLAIN
4280B

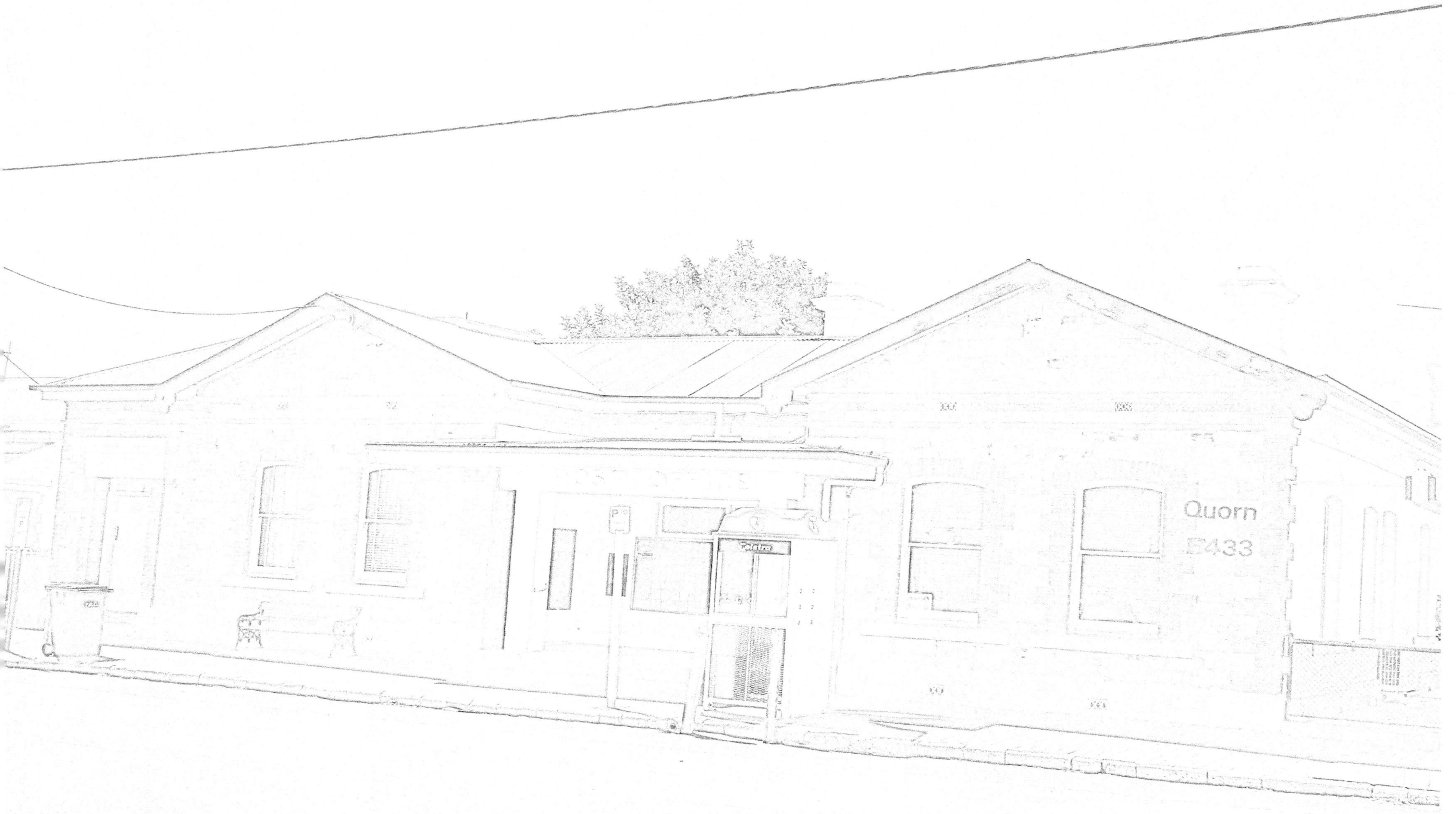
Quorn
5433

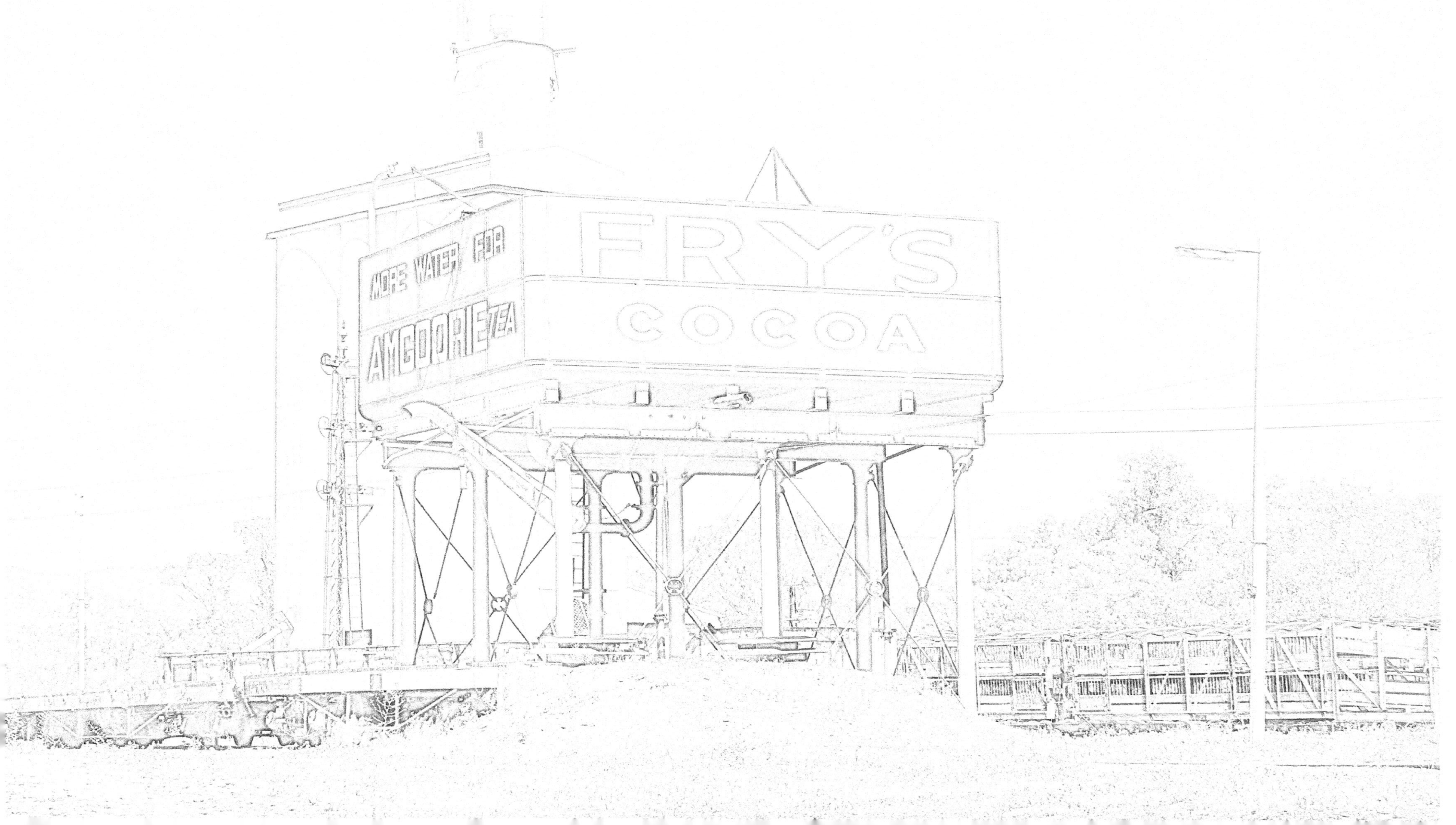
MORE WATER FOR
AMGOORIE TEA
FRY'S
COCOA

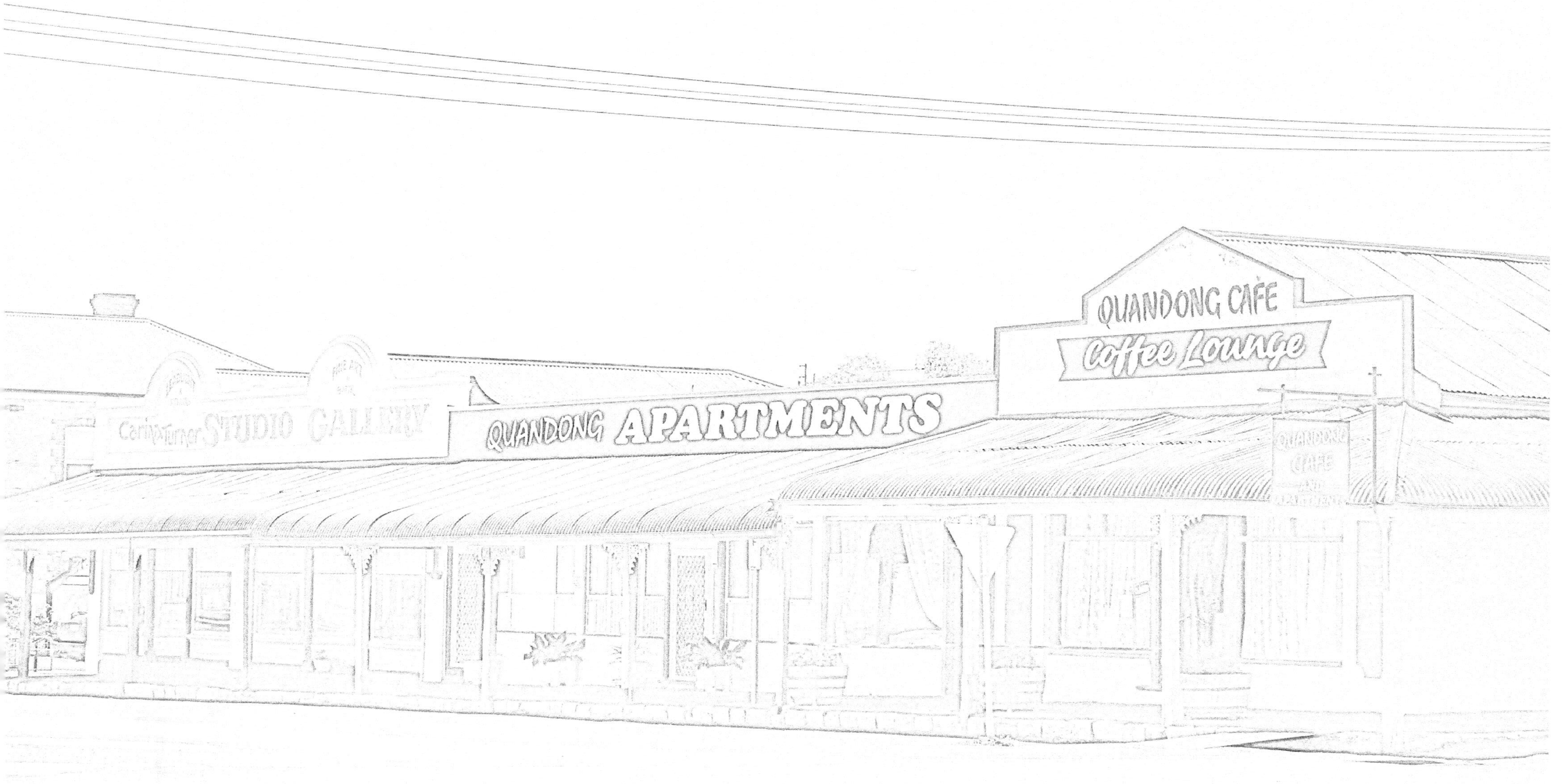
QUANDONG CAFE
Coffee Lounge
QUANDONG APARTMENTS
STUDIO GALLERY

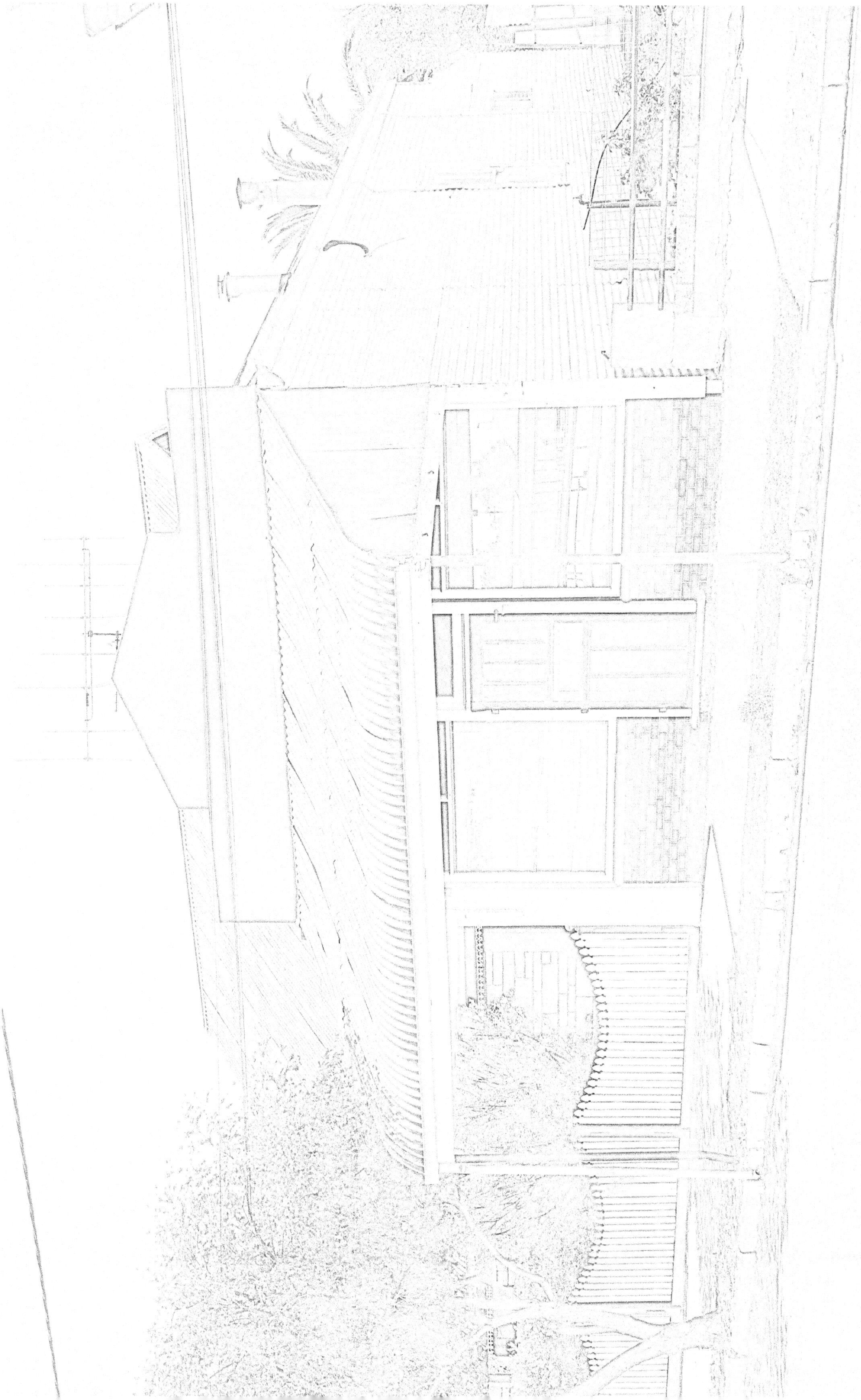

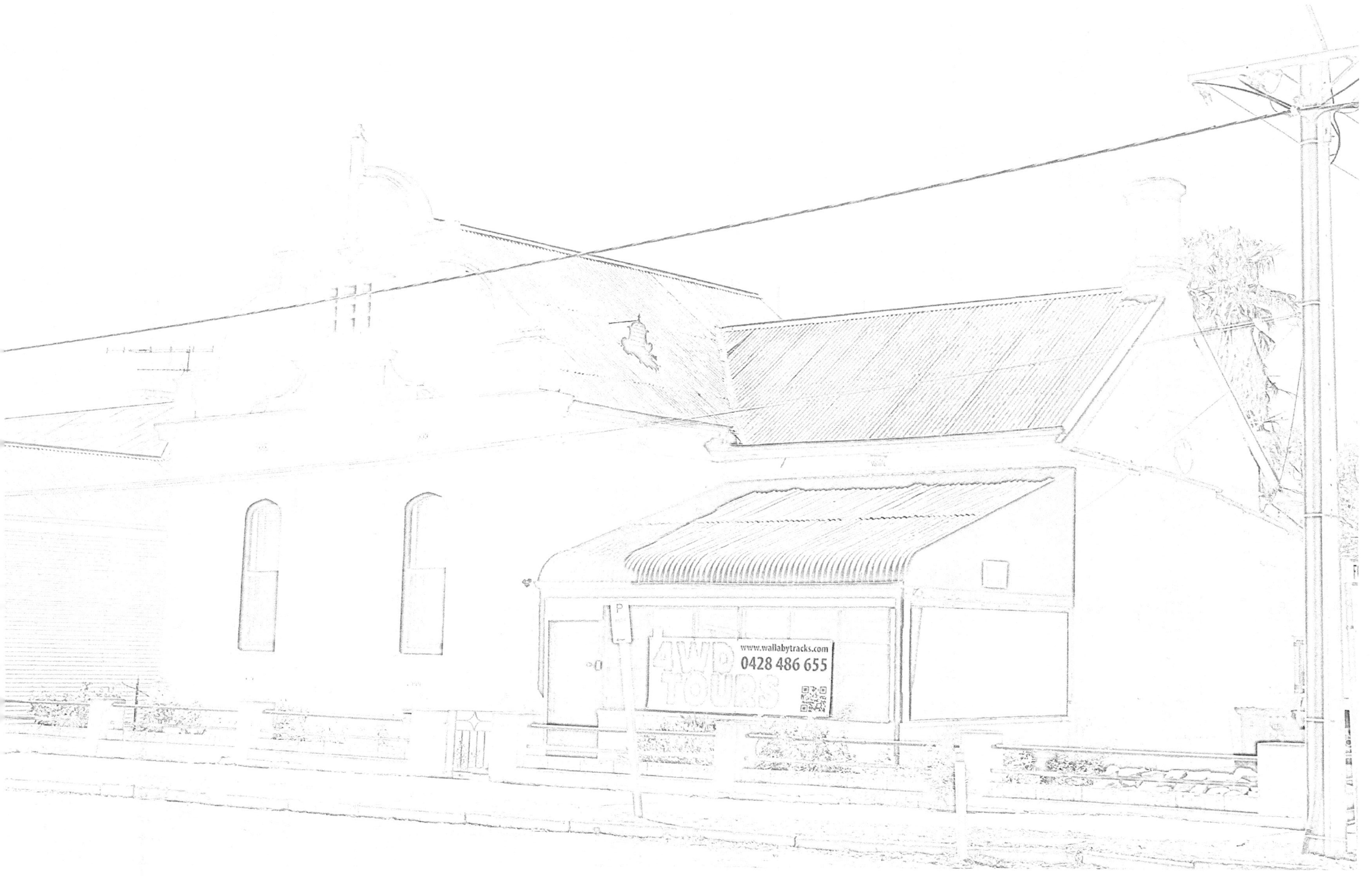
www.wallabytracks.com
0428 486 655
4WD TOURS

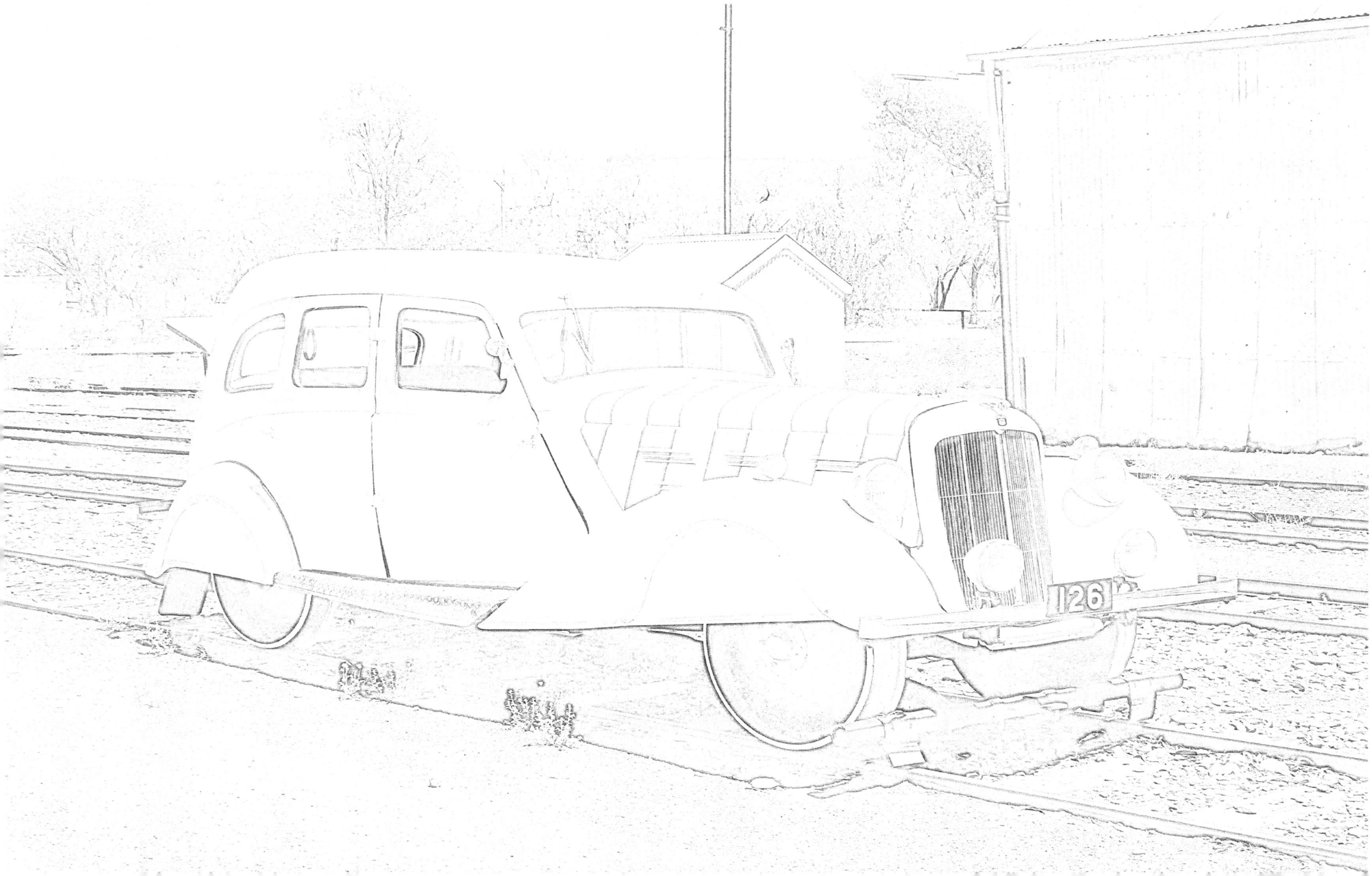
126

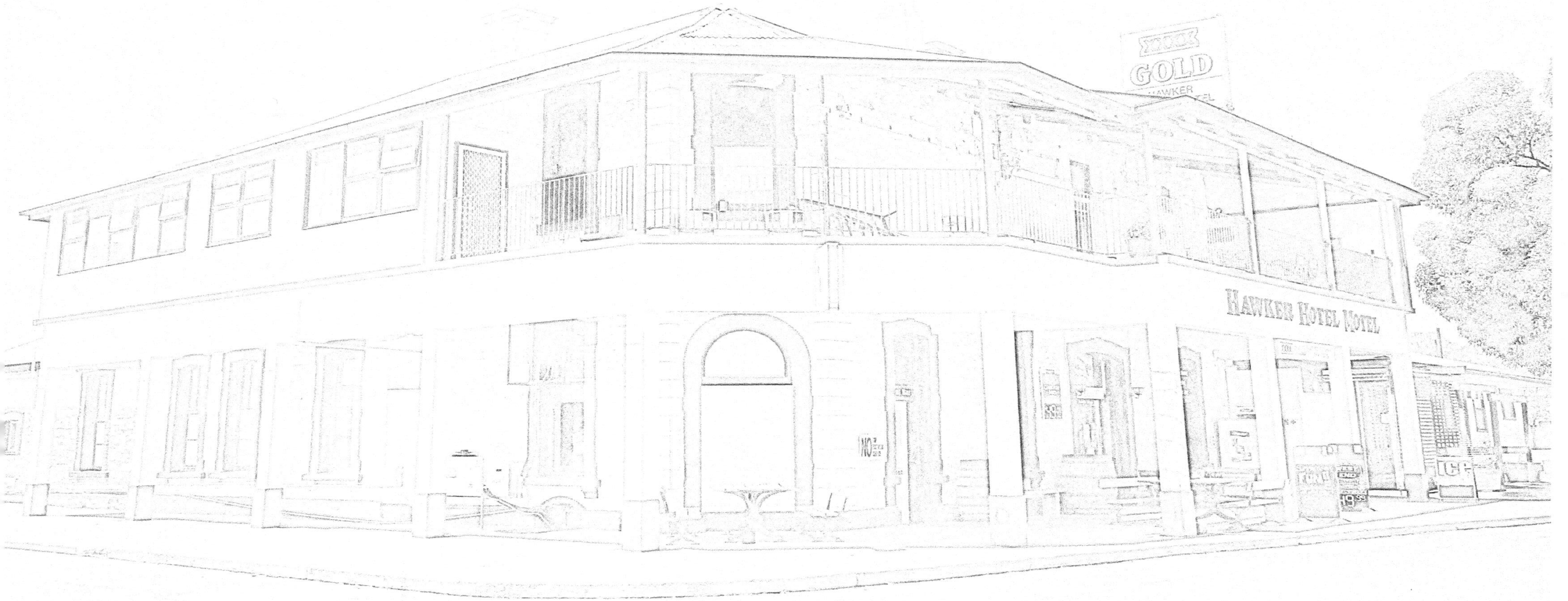
GOLD
HAWKER
HAWKER HOTEL MOTEL
ICE

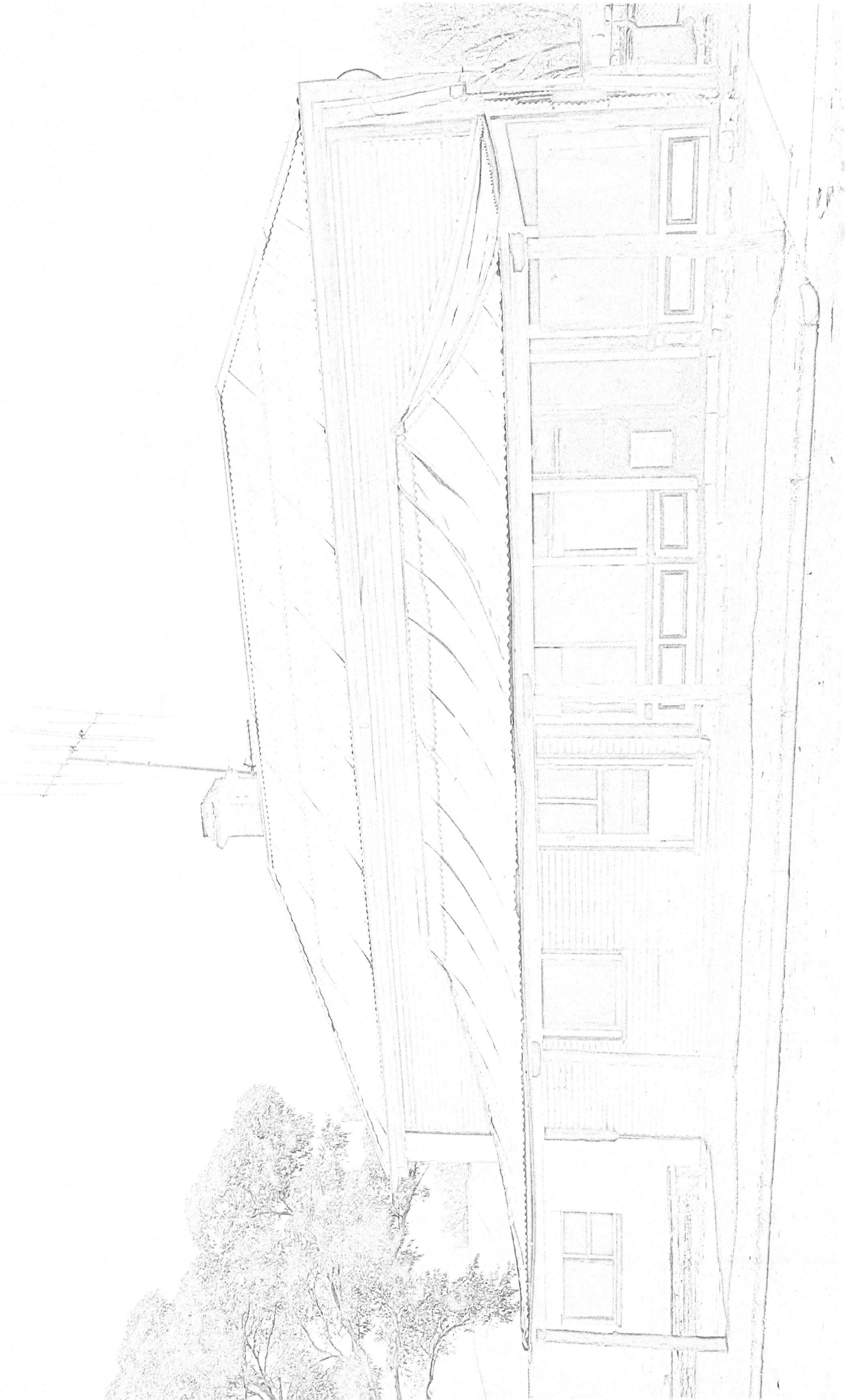

www.ingramcontent.com/pod-product-compliance
Lightning Source LLC
Chambersburg PA
CBHW081100180526
45170CB00005B/1825
9780359972173